Ley
Lines
Across the
Midlands

T0346800

LEY
LINES
ACROSS THE
MIDLANDS

ANTHONY POULTON-SMITH

The
History
Press

First published 2009
Reprinted 2019

The History Press
The Mill, Brimscombe Port
Stroud, Gloucestershire, GL5 2QG
www.thehistorypress.co.uk

© Anthony Poulton-Smith, 2009

The right of Anthony Poulton-Smith to be identified
as the Author of this work has been asserted in accordance
with the Copyrights, Designs and Patents Act 1988.

All rights reserved. No part of this book may be reprinted
or reproduced or utilised in any form or by any electronic,
mechanical or other means, now known or hereafter invented,
including photocopying and recording, or in any information
storage or retrieval system, without the permission in writing
from the Publishers.

British Library Cataloguing in Publication Data.
A catalogue record for this book is available from the British Library.

ISBN 978 0 7509 5051 0

Typesetting and origination by The History Press
Printed in Great Britain by TJ International Ltd, Padstow, Cornwall.

CONTENTS

INTRODUCTION

It was my interest in ley lines which resulted in the eventual books I have written on the origins of place names. Thus it was only a matter of time before I turned my attention to the ancient trackways of England and, in particular here, the Midlands.

Within these pages we will tread the paths walked by our ancestors some 4,000 and more years ago. The routes will take us through some of the loveliest countryside to be found anywhere, some with breathtaking views from the summits of hills down to the valleys below. Sometimes the trackways still pass through woodland, as they did when created to provide safe passage from one hill fort to another.

None of the original markers have survived or, if they have, cannot be shown to be originals. However, the markers which have replaced them are still seen, providing a history lesson everywhere we look: not only cultural history but natural history too, for a wealth of flora and fauna have made these regions their homes. Yet were it not for man's creation of these environments, England would still be one vast woodland: if so many of the plants and animals seen would never have thrived here, whether they had made their own way to our shores or had been introduced by man. This book will have something for those interested in history both ancient and modern, the natural world, walking, or even those who simply delight in this green and pleasant land.

Having walked these ancient paths alone for the most part, I was forced to walk them twice – from the car and back again. However, this provided me with the opportunity to see everything from both aspects, which revealed many things I had not noticed on my outward journey – and these pathways were traversed both ways.

I have no idea how many miles I walked in preparing the following pages, although my level of fitness has improved beyond all expectations. My thanks are due to those who rediscovered the trackways I trod and pointed me in the right direction. Furthermore, without all the establishments that provided a meal for a hungry man and a bed for his very weary legs, I would still be walking today.

To experience the feeling of standing at the site of a hill fort which would have been a hive of activity for centuries was very moving. This path was one which others had walked almost since mankind had first abandoned the life of the hunter-gatherer, forming permanent settlements and adopting the farming life. Images formed of the landscape around me as it would have appeared before Stonehenge and the much earlier Avebury circles were even thought about.

When I walked the land the changing images of Saxon, Romano–British, Iron Age, Bronze Age, and Neolithic times were remarkably easy to see. As you follow my journeys in the ensuing pages I hope you are able to glimpse some of the things I saw.

To follow my footsteps all you require is this book and corresponding Ordance Survey maps.

Anthony Poulton–Smith

CHAPTER ONE

A STRAIGHT LINE

In 1921 Alfred Watkins published a theory. In truth others had had the same idea before, but Mr Watkins was the first to put his thoughts into print. Thus the world was introduced to ley lines.

So what is a ley line? There is some disagreement as to exactly what ley lines are, yet all agree they are lines – and what is more, they are straight lines. Mr Watkins was the first person to give these alignments a name. The word is taken from the Saxon *leah* meaning 'a woodland clearing' and appearing at the end of innumerable place names, such as Hanley, Hinckley, Dudley and Rugeley. However, the accepted pronunciation for the line has become 'lay'. Many cultures have shown an interest in straight lines, the most famous and enduring being the Nazca lines of the high plateau in Peru.

A more recent theory suggests these lines mark the paths of an earth force: intersecting points of two leys are said to release a special psychic or magical energy. This energy is not only said to be beneficial but a vital source of positive energies. There are also those who maintain they are able to trace leys using dowsing rods. I have seen this happen more than once, with different people holding the rods, yet have never managed to get any movement at all from the dowsing rods myself.

Any credence the writer would give to the more supernatural explanation evaporates with the claim that leys can be traced by dowsing, this time using a plumb line over a map. In order to accept that this is possible, we would also have to assume that the tool (either the plumb line or the plumb bob) can read. Otherwise, how would the tool recognise that it was a map – complete with contours, names and features – rather than a piece of paper with a few random letters, and straight and curved lines scribbled on it?

Other properties attributed to leys include the power to heal, a magnetic allure for ghosts and anything supernatural, geomancy, the explanation for the existence and creation of crop circles, and signals to UFOs. There is even an account of an alignment being found on Mars, leading to (or from, depending upon which version you read) the phenomena which has become known as the Face of Mars. Apparently this is the only proof required to show that leys are common to every planet in the galaxy. The author's only acceptance of leys is the same as the man who named them, Alfred Watkins.

Watkins proposed that the straight lines were ancient trackways, laid down by those who settled in the British Isles when it was largely forested. As the ley was created a number of markers were created to enable the traveller to follow the track even though he was out of direct line of sight of both his point of departure and his objective. It is these tracks that this book will be examining.

Obviously the first time anyone travelled from point A to point B there was no marked path to follow. Therefore someone had to find a way of marking the shortest route and also making sure there was no error, otherwise all that was being created was a road to nowhere. The method used to ensure a straight and true path was simplicity itself and the same basic system is still used by surveyors today.

Few tools are required to produce a perfectly straight line over unlimited distances: three wooden staves, in fact, will suffice. Whilst both his point of origin and his target were in sight he would secure his first stake in the ground at a point where it stood on a direct line between the two. The second stake would be placed further along this same line, thus creating two certain points of reference. His third stake would be aligned at a point as far away from the first two as it was possible to see and maintain the accuracy. Now the first stake can be removed and aligned at the front, thus effectively becoming the fourth stake. Alfred Watkins referred to these surveyors as dodmen, citing the gait of the elderly being referred to as 'doddering' and the Welsh *dodi* meaning to place or to lay.

Some have pointed to the staves or stakes being carried by the chalk figure known as the Long Man of Wilmington in Sussex, suggesting the figure may have been created to acknowledge the invaluable contribution these men made. This 69m (227ft) long figure carries two long poles or staves. Like the other human figure of the Giant at Cerne Abbas, these are considered ancient. However, no record of either figure has ever been found dating from before the seventeenth century. Considering the planning and the huge effort which would have gone into the construction, it seems unlikely that either would have avoided any mention for well over 2,000 years.

The only thing left was to create markers. These would have stood out from everything in view like the proverbial sore thumb. Each marker had to be within sight of the previous one as there was no path underfoot to follow. Markers were originally simply a pile of stones, or a burned tree, or a purposely created ford. Later, some of these sites took on more significance and became tumuli, cairns, pagan places of worship and eventually, on occasion, new settlements.

Obviously not all of the permanent markers were contemporary. Indeed, those who doubt the existence of leys point out these great differences in age as evidence that the ley could not have been marked out using the marks cited, for originally many of them could not have existed. This cannot be disputed. However, perhaps the way to look at it is that the markers were erected on the track that was already in existence. Even today any construction work grows alongside an existing road, so it is a safe assumption that this has always been the case. Besides, there would be no point in creating a sacred place which was quite literally off the beaten track where nobody would ever be able to find it.

The Romans, famous for their straight roads, would undoubtedly have taken advantage of the trackways already in existence. They used the same method to mark out their roads which, although they were no wider, were vastly superior underfoot. Furthermore, no markers were required for the road itself was evidence enough. Today these former markers can still sometimes be seen in the names of the settlements; indeed, this is often the only clue we have.

It should be noted that sceptics have discounted the idea of ley lines as fanciful archaeology. Quite rightly they point to the comparatively large number of settlements in Europe and, seeing these as dots on a map, conclude that there is no deliberate alignment.

The fact that there are so many dots means it is inevitable that some will fall in a straight line. Alfred Watkins himself pointed this out in his book *The Old Straight Track*.

This book accepts that ley lines do exist and were marked out. In the following pages you will travel with the author along a number of these ancient routes across the counties of the Midlands. While the different leys have similar markers in a general sense, each has its own individual story to tell and is a different piece of the whole incomplete puzzle; incomplete because the several leys can be traced across distances much greater than just central England. Not only will we discover something of the places and the markers, but will look at the possible reasons and uses for the trackway, and also the people who have followed these same paths.

Although they lie outside the area covered by this book, the stone circles of Avebury and Stonehenge in Wiltshire are well-known as focal points for a number of trackways and, importantly, can be dated. These two religious sites are over 5,000 years old. Clearly they were built on leys that existed before they did, hence the leys themselves are older (and likely much older). Since the original markers have long since disappeared, it is difficult to know exactly when any particular track was created. Indeed it is virtually impossible to say just how old any of the leys are.

Therefore we must guess as to the age of these tracks and for this we need clues. The only ones we have are the people, and when they first settled into permanent homes rather than leading the life of hunter-gatherers. The only other really relevant factor is the forests, which severely hampered the vision of those people of the British Isles and created the need for marked trackways. This all happened about 10,000 years ago.

Whether any of the routes in the succeeding chapters are among the original tracks of 10,000 years ago is unknown and never likely to be known. However it is safe to assume they date from at least the pre-Roman era of 2,000 years ago and are likely to be twice that age.

CHAPTER TWO

THE MARKERS

As mentioned in the first chapter, the existence and recognition of the leys relies on tracing the markers. Clearly the first thing to do is know what we are looking for. Alfred Watkins took a great deal of time and trouble to identify and rate the most common of the markers, his idea being that if an alignment attained a certain score then it was probably the best indicator that a trackway existed. Not a very scientific method maybe, but it must be said to be a fairly accurate one. There are roughly a dozen classical signs which are the first that are looked for. Here we shall examine each one individually.

There can be no doubt the mounds of pre-history are among the most enigmatic and least understood of historical monuments. The tumuli of the Neolithic era were made of stones and posts supporting a covering of earth. These constructions, which contained the remains of their dead, were sometimes huge, measuring 30m (100ft) in width and 150m (500ft) or more in length. The eastern end would be raised and would contain the entrance. Sadly, during the nineteenth century, excavating these ancient sites became very popular with the wealthier classes and, as such, a great deal of damage was done by the so-called barrow-diggers, leaving many more questions unanswered than were ever solved.

Bronze-Age round barrows are the most numerous, with almost 20,000 still found in Britain. Known by a number of different names – including bury, castle, mount, and low – they were built slightly below the actual summit so as to be visible from below. Clearly this suggests the observers must have been now living in the valleys and this dates them as more recent than those built at the summits. During Anglo-Saxon times the round barrow was again briefly popular, until Christianity took hold.

The megalithic tomb was built for exactly the same purpose but clearly involved more planning and forethought than the tumulus. Here a series of chambers and connecting passages allowed ritual burials to be carried out over a long period of time and were clearly constructed to serve for some time. Furthermore, archaeological evidence has shown that these were used for ceremonial purposes, thus the whole should probably be looked upon as a temple.

Another type of mound is the cursus, which is actually a misnomer. These parallel banks with external ditches were thought to be Roman athletics tracks by early British archaeologists and thus described by the Latin *cursus* meaning 'circus'. They actually date from the Neolithic period some 3,000 or more years prior to the Romans and can be anything from 50m (160ft) upwards, with the ends also closed in by earth banks. As these were difficult to recognise, many were demolished by the plough and are now only recognisable from aerial photography and observation.

Cairns are constructed from stones and are Bronze-Age features more often seen in mountainous and moorland areas, where moving vast amounts of earth would pose logistical problems. Dolmens (also known as quoits and cromlechs) are horizontal stone slabs supported by three or more stone pillars. Always thought of as the stone skeletal remains of burial mounds, modern ideas question this, for even if we accept that erosion can take away all the covering soil, it is surely implausible to suggest none of these are found today partially eroded. The term dolmen comes from the Breton *taol maen* meaning 'stone table'; the same meaning from Welsh gives us 'cromlech' and the Cornish word is 'quoit'.

There are also about 100 conical Roman bound barrows in England. While the Roman influence dates much later than the construction of the leys, perhaps we should not be too hasty to dismiss these as possible markers. Archaeologists nearly always find evidence of earlier habitation on the site of more recent activity. It is not impossible that an earlier site lies beneath these Roman mounds, although no evidence has ever been found to support this idea.

Almost without exception the ley itself skirts the sloping sides of the mound, rather than through the centre. This suggests the original construction started to the side of the track, only to cover it when the mound grew in later years.

Mounds are recognised as the most important of markers, simply because of their age and size. Perhaps standing stones, monoliths and markstones would be equally as important (if not more so) were they not so difficult to recognise. While the stones at Avebury could never be seen as anything but man-made, if the circle had been smaller and a number of them had been removed the existence of a large stone may have been given an alternative explanation: indeed, at the boundaries of settlements a large marker stone was very commonly used to mark the boundary between neighbouring parishes.

Later the single large markstone was replaced or maybe added to, forming stone circles, henges, stone rows, or stone crosses. Such large constructions are difficult to date from their beginnings, having assumed greater significance and standing in later times.

While water would doubtless have been used in some respects, the existence of an ancient water site should not be taken as evidence of a ley marker. Ponds and moats should ideally have some secondary pointer of being an early marker. From a distance water would make an ideal marker, for it reflects the natural light from above and would be visible from much further away than a simple pile of stones. Fords are an obvious choice; however, it does help if there is any clue that the river crossing may have been created rather than a natural feature.

It has been noted that the ditch around barrows often does show evidence of having held water. Clearly rain would have had a tendency to accumulate there, yet it may well have been deliberate and for a number of reasons. Water is a natural product and vital to all life, it would also have produced a reflection of the heavens, and a beacon light would have been amplified at night in just the same way as daylight. There is also the term low, which comes from the Anglo-Saxon *hlaew*, speaking of a barrow and also used to mean 'halo'. It is easy to see how a ring of bright water around the site of the temple could resemble a halo. Beacon fires were also important for ley builders as they were visible by night and day, by either flame or smoke.

Ley-line promoter Alfred Watkins gave wells a high rating as a marker. However it is difficult to see how many wells could have been deliberately created as markers on an alignment – though without a well nearby, considerable effort would have been required to transport sufficient water. Therefore it made sense to settle very near or even around the well itself. Obviously a well can only be sunk at certain points and therefore there must be a certain amount of luck involved if a well lies on an alignment, although a well at either the end or beginning of a ley is quite plausible.

Pagan temples and sacred sites are unlikely to be found directly today. Luckily for the ley hunter the oldest of the Christian churches were built upon the former sites of pagan worship. It makes perfect sense to replace the imagery of one religion with that of another on the same site. Thus the conversion to the Christian faith was not limited to the people, but also the temple site too.

Crossroads have often been cited as likely markers, yet the number which can be shown to have existed when leys were marked out are very few and far between. However, meeting points on early trackways were once extremely important places, much as any turning point on modern roads is today.

Roads offer more hope, for if a section of road follows a ley for a significant distance (half a mile or 800m) there is a good chance it is following the line of an ancient ley. The same could also be true of public footpaths and bridleways, providing they can be shown as not being modern creations. Alternatively a road or path may be seen to parallel a ley, in which case it is a safe bet that the road was relocated at some point owing to building or agricultural needs.

Alfred Watkins also gave trees a rating as markers. Now to assume that any tree marker of more than a century ago would still be around today is optimistic in the extreme. However, the name may well still be in existence, as can be seen with 'Ceofa's tree' which is now the city of Coventry – an impossible place to ever attempt to pinpoint the original arboreal marker.

Notches are also named as a probable marker. These are not carved on trees or rocks but are visible only when standing on the ley itself: the notch is in the landscape and will be visible from below the ridge and stand out quite clearly against the skyline. For some reason these features are commonly found along from a ford. However, ensure these are ancient and not where a modern road has been cut.

Camps or hill forts are predictable sights when walking leys. It is highly unlikely that these were the original marker, but probably grew from an earlier (and now unknown) marker. Such sites are particularly evident where two or more leys cross or converge. One of the best examples is the British Camp on the Malvern Hills.

CHAPTER THREE

St Bertram's Well to Tup Low

This ley runs for approximately 40km from near Ilam in Staffordshire, a little east of directly north into Derbyshire. The well of St Bertram lies on the west side of Bunster Hill overlooking the village of Ilam. There is a footpath leading there along the side of the hill from the Izaak Walton Hotel. This is no walk for the unfit: this is a substantial ascent and should not be attempted unless properly equipped and in reasonably fit condition. The well is approximately 200m above sea level, while the top of the hill towers more than another 100m above us.

This is not the only ancient site dedicated to this particular saint: St Bertram's Bridge crosses the River Manifold just south of Ilam. Bertram, sometimes known as Bettelin, is thought to have been an eighth-century Saxon king of Mercia. Tradition holds he travelled to Ireland seeking religious enlightenment, only to meet and fall in love with a beautiful princess. Together they returned to Mercia and lived in the forest around Stafford where she gave birth. One day, while Bertram was out hunting, wolves visited their shelter and killed his beloved wife and their newborn child. Grief-stricken, Bertram shunned his royal ancestry and dedicated his life to God. He approached the royal court in disguise and managed to acquire a grant of land for his hermit's retreat.

The new king followed no religion, so as soon as he heard of the hermitage (which has been recorded as Bethnei) he demanded the land be returned to the Crown. Eventually it was decided that the decision be made by personal combat, a common solution for a difficult disputed decision of the day. Bertram appealed to God for assistance and, when a dwarf came forward, he was reminded of the Bible story of David and Goliath and so allowed the dwarf to fight in his stead. Victory for the quick and agile dwarf allowed Bertram to keep the land.

Retiring to his hermitage proved a mistake. Rather than solitude, Bertram received a stream of visitors seeking his help in their search for spiritual enlightenment. Thus the former king was forced to seek an alternative hideout, eventually reaching a cave near the present well which bears his name. Although there is a shrine in the local parish church to St Bertram, the well is little more than a few stones forming a semi-circle where a natural spring emerges from the hillside.

St Bertram's Well on Dunster Hill.

A lovely view from Dunster Hill towards Ilam.

From the holy well the footpath continues north where it intersects another; turn right and ascend a very tough path almost to the summit 300m above sea level. Follow the field boundary north to Ilam Tops Farm then sharp right, down to where this path follows the upper edge of Dovedale Wood north. Eight hundred metres along here the path descends through the woodland.

While the path follows the easier route, the ley follows a straight course across Ilam Tops to the west bank of the River Dove. Here a footbridge enables us to cross the most scenic of rivers, where originally the traveller would have forded the swiftly flowing stream – not a pleasant prospect in the depths of winter when the river was in spate. Looking straight ahead we see Dove Holes and Shining Tor beyond, where the river once again meets up with the ley (although this time touched by the opposite bank). The easier walk today follows the river until reaching Coldeaton when the main river turns west while we continue north along the valley known as Biggin Dale.

As the terrain becomes comparatively less rugged the path separates between Ferny Bottom and Biggin Grange. Take the path to the east and ascend to meet Liffs Road, where we turn left, and 400m along (right across the field) pass the Waterloo public house. To the east we can see the church at Biggin: dedicated to St Thomas, it is one of very few buildings in a small village. This place of worship is the venue of a flower festival held every July and, despite its appearance, only dates from the middle of the nineteenth century.

Follow the footpath as it swings gently north-west towards Chapel Farm and then almost doubles back on itself. Within 200m turn left and cross the Tissington Trail, a popular route used by walkers and cyclists alike. The footpath continues north and then skirts Ruby Wood around to the west. Turn right at the lane heading past the quarry and, at the junction, turn first right and then left on the A515, the major road through the Peak District here. At the crossroads with Green Lane, these days little more than a track, we are once again on the path of the ley.

Current routes have made crossing to the next marker impossible, thus we are forced to follow the A515 Buxton Road north, turning right on to The Rakes, and right again on to Long Rakes. Here we travel back along the track marked by English Heritage to view Arbor Low, one of the most complete and impressive megalithic sites in Derbyshire.

If we walked the exact line – which is neither practical nor recommended – it would take us close to a tumulus at End Low, east of Ruby Wood. Through the aforementioned crossing (the A515, where it forms a crossroads with Green Lane), there is another tumulus to our right and slightly behind us, while to the left the track that is Green Lane takes us to two other burial mounds including Moneystones. Meanwhile the ley forges ever onward across the High Peak Trail/Pennine Bridleway, depending on your mode of transport, and crosses a former Roman road by the now disused Blakemoor Pits. Signs of the road surface still remain almost 2,000 years after it was constructed. We shall visit the High Peak Trail and the Roman road in chapter 24.

Shortly afterwards it passes Gib Hill and yet another tumulus. However, it is the name of the hill which will evoke greater feelings. It refers to this being the place where at least one murderer was hanged in the eighteenth century. Pausing to look, it is easy to image this scene silhouetted against the skyline. A curving bank connects this site with the better known site which is the next marker.

Our target is the major sighting on this ley and the most important stone circle in this part of England. Arbor Low features over forty blocks of local limestone forming a henge on top of an oval bank 83m at its widest point and over 2m high, with a smaller tumulus. The blocks form an egg-shaped ring and today lie flat: indeed, there is no evidence to suggest they ever stood. Limestone erodes comparatively quickly and the blocks are showing obvious signs of having remained on this open windswept moorland almost

Arbor Low with Gib Hill in
the centre background.

400m above sea level for 5,000 years.

Both the Arbor Low and Gib Hill barrows contain human ashes. Covered in stones
on the east side of the feature was a male skeleton. This was assumed to be a ritual burial,
possibly sacrificial, as no finery was found with the remains. Before leaving Arbor Low
take a look back along the ley and, when the conditions are optimum, a constructed or
worn entranceway can be seen aligned perfectly with the ley.

Making our way back to Long Rake we turn right. Four hundred metres along here
a footpath leads north-east along a dip to Cales Farm and beyond, across Cales Dale and
north to One Ash Grange Farm. Turn left here along Limestone Way to Monyash, where
we emerge on to Derby Lane leading to Rakes Road and then across the crossroads and
north along Chapel Street. Turning right we walk along Horse Lane and then right along
an unnamed lane to a three-way road junction. Arriving here we are standing on the
alignment once more and take the unnamed road north-west.

Turn left along Flagg Lane at the next junction and 800m later turn right along Wheal
Lane, little more than a track here. Another 400m along and we divert right and continue
down Deep Dale. Eventually we shall arrive at the public car park alongside the A6 at
Lees Bottom. Continue along the valley following the River Wye upstream northwards

The views over Monsal Head Dale are breathtaking whatever the season.

towards Monsal Dale. As the course of the river and the footpath we are following sweeps to the right, above us across the river on this corner is Monsal Dale and the next marker on the ley.

To have followed the trackway over this ridge was too much on the day I walked the ley: indeed, I would warn anyone to seriously consider this walk before attempting it. The walk along the course of the river is certainly most enjoyable. However, I did return at a later date solely to come up here to enjoy the views which were obviously awaiting me.

The next target here is the originally Bronze-Age settlement nestled alongside Fin Cop. Defensive banks and ditches to the south and east are plainly visible, while the natural feature of Monsal Dale protects the other two sides. Local folklore maintains spending the night here will drive one insane. However, it is worthwhile pausing here to take in the view – Kinder Scout is said to be visible on a clear day – before continuing on to our next stop.

Before long this view of Monsal Dale centres on the viaduct. Built in the 1860s to carry the Midland Railway between Matlock and Buxton, this five-arched construction only serves to add to the vista. The track was removed some time ago and now serves walkers and cyclists as part of the Monsal Trail.

The views across the Wye Valley are breathtaking at any time of the year. However we must eventually cross to the other side and to the Monsal Head Hotel. From here we take Castlegate Lane north where, 2km away, just past the milestone and Rolley Low, a lane heads back up the hill to a car park at Upperdale Farm. To the north of the car park is a tumulus at Hay Top, the next marker on the ley. Again this would have meant a most strenuous climb from the Wye Valley; thus I visited on another day when the car took much of the work.

Excavations of this almost circular burial mound, measuring 20m in diameter and 1.3m maximum height, uncovered three quite separate internments. Here were found a variety of human bones, arrowheads, jars, beads and two intact skulls. It is only a few metres from another point which has been cited as a potential marker, that of Moss Well.

The journey along the ley continues from the junction at Castlegate Lane; turn right along the same track and follow it to Longstone Moor and then north to the junction with Thunderpit Lane – and finally the A623, 2km away. We now face right and, in 100m, turn left to Foolow some 700m away. At the junction turn left and head towards Grindlow. Just over 600m along here we reach the final ley marker, the tumulus known as Tup Low.

This was undoubtedly the most strenuous of the walks. However, it also afforded the best views and the wildest scenery. It paid to pause and remember that this was a route used during the Bronze Age, when many of the modern paths and bridges simply did not exist. It was certainly a sobering thought to remember that not only did these people walk the route in a straight line, but also whilst carrying the goods they were hoping to trade or had traded.

Obviously these individuals were strong, very fit and appreciated a beautiful walk.

CHAPTER FOUR

BEACON HILL TO OADBY

Not all leys forge a straight line through what remains of England's wildernesses. Once these trackways linked the major population centres, so we should not be too surprised to find a ley forging its way straight through a major city; the only surprise is that the ley can still be traced under the concrete of modern society.

In order to trace this ancient track we must start outside the city of Leicester to the north-west. Bradgate Park is not only 350 hectares of ancient deer park and the birthplace of Lady Jane Grey, but is the setting for the folly known as Old John's Tower. It is a fairly modest construction as follies go, just two storeys high, but at over 170m above sea level it affords magnificent views around the Leicestershire countryside.

It was not built as a ley-line marker, of course. Indeed, the construction only dates from the eighteenth century when, according to some reports, it allowed ladies a view of the racecourse which circled the top of this hill. A rough circle of stones surrounds this hill – could they have marked out the course? The arch, which makes this one of the county's most easily recognised sights (making the silhouette on the skyline look not unlike a very large beer mug), was added in 1786.

Originally this was the site of an old windmill belonging to Old John, in turn becoming the name of the present building. Legend has it that this employee of the 5th Earl of Stamford was killed in quite unusual circumstances. It seems that a party was being held to mark the twenty-first birthday of the earl's son. A rather boisterous male assemblage seemed to think it would be a good idea to build a bonfire around the flagpole there. Sadly, when the fire started it brought the pole crashing down upon the unfortunate Old John, killing him instantly – a highly fanciful tale probably created to explain the name and with no basis in truth.

However, this is not the start of the ley. From here it is quite easy to see the beginning to the north-west: indeed it is difficult to miss the 245m high Beacon Hill, the site of a Bronze-Age hill fort and the second highest point in the county. No obvious signs of the ancient settlement remain; however, there is a small toposcope. Here a brass plate sits on top of a stone plinth, the radiating lines showing points of interest visible in that direction (including Old John's Tower). It is claimed that Lincoln Cathedral is visible from this point,

Old John's Tower on Beacon Hill.

yet even though it was the clearest of days I could not make out the building with its two great towers standing high above the surrounding city.

Beacon Hill is not just an ancient sighting point: it also has what has become known as a 'trig pillar' – short for triangulation pillar. Standing around 1m high, these concrete markers are found dotted throughout the country and were erected to support a theodolite. Every single pillar was designed to be visible from two others, hence the triangle, and are placed on the highest point in the area. Today it is often only possible to see one other point, but it is perhaps no surprise to find how often they stand on, or very close to, an ancient ley. By using these, detailed and remarkably accurate maps of Britain were produced. While the modern global positioning systems are undoubtedly more accurate, they are only marginally so and are simply easier to read than basic maps.

Each of these pillars carries a unique number and there are a number of slightly different designs despite the basic shape, making collection of their designation and a photograph (with the collector, of course) an unusual hobby. At one time there were over 6,000 of these dotted around the country, around 70 per cent of which still survive.

Extending the line south-east between the two we find we eventually close in on Bradgate Road just as it is entering Anstey. To the north of this road, the final three fields prior to the houses exhibit signs of earlier habitation. The unmistakable signs of an earlier settlement can be seen from aerial photographs. It is thought that this represents elements from a number of historical periods, although without recent field archaeology it is impossible to say when the earliest settlers arrived.

The very name of Anstey may well be a clue to the existence of a ley, for it has been defined as '(place at) the narrow path'. If further evidence is required there is also a path which is still sometimes referred to locally as The Leys.

A little further along the 16km course the ley hits two makers in the village of Anstey, frequently referred to as 'the Gateway to the Forest' (i.e. Charnwood). The Church of St Mary comes first, the oldest parts of which are known to date from 1220. That Christian places of worship replaced former pagan sites is certain. Indeed it is likely the mandate from the Vatican was not 'convert the people', when envoys were sent to England, but 'convert their places of worship'.

Just a little further on near Gynsall Lane and alongside the A46 is Anstey Stone. For as long as anyone could remember the stone was horizontal until a local farmer stood it on its end, returning it to its former position rising 2m above the surrounding land.

One of the major road junctions in the area is next, the roundabout where the A50 meets the A453. Once a crossroads and lying directly on the ley, the meeting of Glenfrith Way and New Parks Way with the Groby Road has appeared on maps for centuries – although not until recently were they so named!

Following the ley line we rejoin the A50 trunk road at Frog Island. The name suggests one thing but is clearly not an island as we would know it. However, in times past it may well have been an effective island as it was (at least for the majority of the time) an isolated patch of dry land bordered by the River Soar to the north and surrounded by marshland. The exact site of this dry land coincides with the ley line and its (now) well hidden marker stone.

The ley also crosses the site of the Britella plastics factory on Frog Island. As mentioned in the first chapter there are those who consider ley lines a magnet for ghosts, and doubtless the workers at that factory during the 1970s would agree. Unexplained damage to machinery and feelings of cold so unnerved the workers they demanded an exorcism be performed or industrial action would be taken.

Just further along we come to All Saint's Church, a fourteenth-century building which, along with the adjoining roads, was declared a conservation area in 1999. However, it may be argued that it is not the church that is the marker but High Cross Street which runs alongside, the name adding weight to this argument. It should be noted that while the church is probably the stronger marker, it may not have been built on the exact site of the original pagan temple and thus the road name is the more likely marker.

Quite a jump to the final marker, 6km to the fourteenth-century Oadby Church of St Peter's. Such a distance may seem to make the suggestion of this being on the ley a little hard to believe. Yet we should remember that this part of Leicester is heavily populated, and has been for many years, so any markers laid down centuries ago will have been decimated.

Today the steeple is still visible from quite a distance and there is no doubt it is still the local landmark. In fact, nothing is likely to have stood out more since the monks built the first known chapel on this site in 1075. This seems an unusual point for the terminus of the ley; however, there are no modern signs of a continuation. It is possible it joins another here which followed the general line of the modern A6. Either way, this 16km track packs a lot of history into its short course.

Admittedly I was not expecting this walk to be among the most enjoyable as it passes right through the centre of the city of Leicester. Not that I have anything against this city: simply that it is less punishing to walk across farmland than concrete. However, I was pleasantly surprised and time passed remarkably quickly.

It was indeed a most pleasant day.

St Peter's Church, Oadby.

CHAPTER FIVE

CROFT AMBREY TO STRETTON GRANDISON

As discussed in the opening chapter, the ley line was first put into print by Alfred Watkins in his book *The Old Straight Track*. As the realisation of what he was seeing dawned on him he had discovered the first ley line. It is only fitting that we walk this very same path trodden almost a century earlier by Alfred Watkins, for without him this book would not have been written and you would not be reading it.

While Watkins rode through the area around Blackwardine (where he marked out this first ley), this author began his trek at the northernmost point and walked the 27km south-south-east from Croft Ambrey to Stretton Grandison. Despite being over 3,000 years old, the grandeur and strength of the beginning of our trek remains quite obvious. The ditches and ramparts are still remarkably clear and the whole site is an impressive thirteen hectares. From the highest point, at around 300m above sea level on the ridge near Mortimer's Cross, it has been said there are views to fourteen counties. Standing here we see sufficiently interesting history all around without even casting our eyes to what lies below.

This Iron-Age hill fort has seen several stages of development. From the earliest beginnings it grew until, by the fifth century BC, there was a village of several rows of rectangular houses built from wood. A century later an annexe was constructed which more than doubled the size of the area, although this addition was probably solely for their livestock, sheep and cattle. Archaeologists have studied the enclosure and evidence has been found suggesting that, at the height of its occupancy, there were at least 500 individuals here. However, the true figure may well have been almost twice this number.

A natural triangular shape affords good protection to the north with its steep slopes. A massive inner rampart, together with outer banks, ditches, walls and gates made this a formidable defensive structure. It remained so until the place was destroyed around AD 48, probably by the Romans, although their victory was never recorded. Just one further development occurred around the end of the second century, when a mound was built, thought to have been a sanctuary of some pre-Christian religious significance. Altogether there have been at least fifteen quite different periods of construction discerned by archaeologists.

Leaving Croft Ambrey we follow the Mortimer Trail, a 50km path across ridges and uplands named because it once belonged to the Mortimer family, north-east around the approximate line of the 270m contour. At the spring on top of the ridge, where the stream cuts down through Lady Wood, we follow the path alongside it. This brings us down into the Fishpool Valley where we come within 50m of the ley once more.

Eventually the footpath curves around and out of the woodland on to Green Lane where, at the Old Rectory, we turn right and follow the road. This takes on a journey almost parallel to the ley and into Yarpole and the Bell Inn. The village's most precious historical treasure is also one of the tallest. The main body of the church is entirely separate from the bell tower and is one of the few remaining timber-framed buildings in the country, dendro-dating putting its construction at around 1192.

By now we are some 800m from the ley line. This cannot be avoided as around this part of the journey there are few roads and footpaths and the pathways leading down from the hills above the village of Croft take us away from it. We could have turned west at Cock Gate and travelled along the B4362 and then along Croft Lane, thereafter making the walk much closer to the original ley. However, the alternative route does not offer any markers or better views – it is simply closer – so I decided to take the shorter path instead.

Green Lane cuts right through Yarpole where, shortly after the Church of St Leonard, we turn right and follow this lane down to the crossroads at Bicton. Today the crossroads is approximately 20m from the ley but has probably slipped a little to the east over the centuries. For a track to wander is not unusual, especially in the days when it was a simply a dirt track which would cut up badly in wet weather. Without hedgerows to channel the traffic, as it were, there was a tendency to take the drier line where the grass had not been worn away, much as we often did when walking the footpaths across the Midlands during the early twenty-first century.

Turn left at the crossroads and follow Croft Lane south-east. As with the crossroads, much of the next 2km of this lane is so close to the original track we can consider it to be aligned. Our journey along the next 4km is largely uneventful, as little remains of markers which must have once existed along the ridges. However, if we continue to check our progress on the map we will discover some most interesting and unusual place names.

Examples of such names include The Riddle and Little Crows, which lie either side of the lane approximately 1km from Bicton shortly before we cross the Herefordshire Trail, a modern pathway we shall encounter again. Soon afterwards, when the road makes a minimal turn to the right, are a few buildings in the region known as Lydiates. Crossing Eyton Lane to our right is an area known as Lydiatts and 600m along, where a footpath meets Croft Lane from the north, is another area also known as Lydiatts. The three names all refer to 'the grey ridge' and, while they have no relevance to the route we are following, it is so highly unusual to find three places with near identical names in such close proximity it is worth noting – and they are really identical, despite one having a slightly different spelling. On the subject of unusual names, as we descend the hill to the left, opposite a few farm buildings, is an area known as Scatterbrain.

As we reach the junction the Herefordshire Trail reappears: follow this to and across the junction, where it is known as The Broad. The Trail is well marked as it leads around the field boundaries east, south and then south-east to bring us to the A44 on the outskirts of Leominster. We need this to help take us across both the railway and the River Lugg. There is a crossing point further south, but it takes us away from the mark point which would undoubtedly have once stood on Eaton Hill.

Instead, follow the Herefordshire Trail to Mill Street, turn left and, immediately over the river, turn right along the footpath leading directly towards Eaton Hill. Note while the first 500m is as flat as any this book encounters, there is a climb of 50m up to the summit of the hill which lies directly on the original alignment. The footpath takes us along the ridge to eventually rejoin the A44, here known as the Worcester Road, which we follow until turning right along Stretford Road towards Blackwardine. There is a footpath which would take us away from the road in the general direction of Stoke Prior. However, no advantage could be seen if this route was followed – it has no obvious markers and would have served only to complicate the route – so I decided to follow the roadway for the purposes of this guide.

Stretford Road runs to Stretford north of us here. Any road named such is a Roman road and here crossed a ford. Oddly the river which was forded is now known as the Stretford Brook, a process known as back-formation, while the original name of the river has been lost. The former Roman road does not have any relevance to this trackway, although it is quite possible it was constructed along an earlier trackway.

Crossing the line of the dismantled railway from the crossroads we reach the ancient settlement site of Blackwardine. The most important relic as far as we are concerned is the mark stone, which marks a very important site even it is unlikely to be the original stone. Suggestions of tests to show how long this stone has been here are pointless. The whole site underwent major disturbance when the railway came through here in the nineteenth century and the marker stone is certainly not in its original position.

Many finds have been uncovered in what has become the line of the railway track: Samian pottery shards from the first century, a Roman coin from the time of Hadrian, another dated AD 87 and a third AD 322, fragments of glass and tiles all lend weight to the argument that this was an important Roman base during the period when Ostorius Scapula led the advance force of legions into the west of England from about AD 48.

Even more telling are the personal items found here, notably the bracelet and ring of gold and a significant number of human bones. What is known is that this was the Romano-British settlement known as Black Caer Dun.

Unfortunately, what little excavation has taken place has been badly recorded and, without further archaeological evidence, it is almost impossible to draw any real conclusions. What is certain is that Blackwardine must have been an important sighting point on the trackway and the place is probably of lesser importance today than it has been ever since the area was first settled.

Having crossed the summit and started to descend, a road joins from the right and the footpath we require is directly opposite. Follow this straight ahead for 700m to where the paths cross and take the right-hand path. This takes us toward Risbury Camp; we pass the site of Gob's Castle shortly before reaching the top of the rise. Clearly this is a personal name used as a place name, although today it seems unlikely anyone would be tempted to christen their child this!

This was the most pleasant stretch of the ley to walk and brings us to Risbury Camp. Today the site has many deciduous trees growing here. While the extensive root system may be seen as invasive, even destructive, in truth it has served to protect the fortification together with canopy. The lack of erosion is noticeable, particularly to the south. Of course the trees also make it harder to see the overall picture, but partial glimpses of the various sections tend to make the observer concentrate on details.

More than ten hectares in total, the central oval of four hectares of flat ground is surrounded by a *vallum* and *fosse*. A natural water defence is created on three sides by the confluence of the Humber Brook with the Holly Brook. Beneath the overhanging branches of the orchard to the west is a quite obvious channel. This is all that remains of the mill fleet which would have allowed water from the Holly Brook to feed the mill pond and power the former watermill before being returned to the Humber Brook. The mill pond is hardly recognisable today, having silted up many years ago.

The worn path is discernable, with Risbury Camp behind the wood to the left.

Walking away from the camp I met with someone from Risbury Court Farm who told me, as we watched the buzzards circling over the ancient site, that these were not the only wildlife seen regularly here. Aside from the usual foxes, rabbits and often-seen birds, there are glimpses of skylarks, hare, muntjack and roe deer, while at night owls and bats patrol the skies seeking their chosen prey.

Continue along the path past the mill to Risbury Bridge. The ley continues on along its unerring course yet modern field boundaries and pathways here run the opposite way and we are forced to take a detour some way away from the straight line. Follow the Bowley Lane south-east, sticking always to the main road as it turns to head south. As we cross Butford Brook, glance to the left and note Wood Farm 500m to the east. In no way can this be considered a marker but it is given as a point of reference to keep the original route and our path in perspective. This is important, for we are going to be straying almost 2km from the ideal line.

A kilometre after crossing the brook we pass the estate of Broadfield Court. Mentioned in the Domesday Book, this is forty hectares of farming country with its own vineyard and winery producing acclaimed wines. The house dates from the sixteenth century and is a venue for a number of corporate events and also for many weddings.

After 4km along Bowley Lane we come to the oddly named Isle of Rhea and, at the junction, Saffron's Cross – which is certainly nothing to do with the priceless spice but most likely a corrupted personal name. Turn left at the junction along the A417 and from here the distance between the two routes will be gradually reduced. Two kilometres from the junction there is a small river passing under the road; the ravine down which the stream flows runs down from a flat-topped hill between Old Coppice and Dudale's Wood. This would have been an ideal site for a marker, or more likely two, one either side of the summit.

Three kilometres further along we come to Cornett Bridge. Pause here and look to the left and almost directly north of the road. There is a well-defined line heading away up the slopes which is the edge of Combs Hill Wood and the aptly named Long Wood; alongside is a summit which forms a quite obvious round but small peak which is exactly on the alignment. Doubtless this would have been a natural marker which would have been accentuated by utilising a pile of stones or similar long-lasting mark.

About 500m after Cornett Bridge there is a lane leading off to the left. It is said to be Hope Lane by some documents, though there was no obvious name to be seen as I turned along it. Two hundred metres along the road bends sharply to the left; we must continue straight ahead along the tree-lined path for a further 400m. It was my intention to continue a further 200m and take the path heading south, but I was unable to locate the route and doubled back instead, effectively taking the road heading south toward Upper Town.

At the junction turn left along Wilden Bank and head east for 800m. Climbing the slope there is a footpath off to the left which is a little difficult to find. There is a second path 200m further on which leads to the same place which is much easier to find, but entails climbing higher up the hill. The first path passes through the wood in a straight line: when it turns right and begins to descend we are crossing the alignment but cannot see along the line for the trees.

Emerging from Derndale Coppice the path heads south to Burley Gate, visible just over a kilometre away. We arrive at a dog-leg along the A465 and walk the 50m or so south to where the path takes us off to the left and on a loop around Long Coppice to return to the route of the A417 once more. This will only be a walk of 600m along this road; we will soon be turning across country, but it is necessary to avoid detouring too far away to the east and increasing the distance substantially.

There are two footpaths to the left and we must be careful not to take the first one, which will only lead us back north. This incorrect path lies exactly opposite the road to Ocle Pychard and is literally only a footpath. We will take the second, a lane quite capable of taking a vehicle. Seven hundred metres along here, shortly before Cowarne Court, we cross the ley line once more (although there is little in the way of natural markers to show the position other than a small pond to the north which is almost impossible to see from ground level as it surrounded by greenery).

Follow the path past the next copse and it turns towards the south again, thus avoiding a rise directly in our path. Here we are taken down a barely discernable slope toward Eggleton, a walk of over a kilometre which takes us across the A4103 and on to Stretton Gransdison, which is as yet still hidden by the rise between. It may be worthwhile pausing at the main road to look west where, some 200m away, there is a footbridge which stands on the alignment. Again it is not suggested as a marker; the watercourse can almost be leapt – it is that narrow – and would have been forded, but is given simply as a reference point. There is no point in walking back as visibility along the alignment is poor.

Thus continuing onward we climb a slope to skirt Stretton Coppice and then upward to the 100m-high summit at Stretton Grandison where the path descends straight toward the Church of St Lawrence. This is not on the line but some 40m west of it. On reaching the road turn left and shortly afterwards there is a building on our left: this is the vicarage, and where the drive meets the road is the next reference point.

However, we must continue along a further 100m and take the footpath off to the right. On reaching the lane take the footpath directly opposite to the end and there turn right. This leads us towards the very visible Church of St James at Canon Frome, home to several memorials to the Hopton family who were lords of this manor until 1947. Skirting the lake we divert and then reach the lane. Turn right here and 100m along there is a crossroads formed by two tracks intersecting at right angles. This is as close as we can reach today to the site where this original ley of Alfred Watkins terminates.

The former Roman station of Stretton Grandison has been largely overlooked for a long time. Recent aerial photographs are aiding archaeologists as they are discovering this was a sizable walled town. Furthermore, although little field work has been done here, this ten hectare site is thought to date from early in the Roman era.

It probably dates from AD 47 or 48, when it would have been an important station during the early campaigns of the governor, Publius Ostorius Scapula. The encampment was protected by a double rampart and ditch system, with evidence of gateways to the east and west. Within the buildings would have faced west towards Wales; it was a garrison for 500 men, probably a mix of foot soldiers and cavalry or *cohors equitata quingenaria*.

That the importance of this site has been misinterpreted is further evidenced by the auxiliary fort on the south bank of the River Frome. This stood directly opposite the civilian settlement on the north bank, some 400m east from where the Roman road forded the river leading south to Dymock.

In a direct line this would have been a walk of less than 30km; effectively this was a walk of almost twice that spread over three days. Of all the walks this was among the most tiring: it certainly tested the stamina with its many undulations. Little of the route could be walked directly – aside from the alignment along Croft Lane we only managed to cross the original pathway. However, to have walked the original path described by Alfred Watkins was a rewarding experience.

CHAPTER SIX

HAUNTON TO
BURTON HASTINGS

We begin our journey in the tiny Staffordshire village of Haunton in the valley of the River Mease. Ahead of us lay a 27km journey south-east to Burton Hastings in Warwickshire.

The day was a pleasant one, summer was still vividly in the memory and autumn had yet to truly show itself in the landscape. However, from the aptly named Pear Tree Cottage, Haunton, a huge bag of this same fruit departed in the car which had brought us here – minus a few choice examples to help fuel our journey.

The starting point is St Michael and St James, a Catholic church, where the Sisters of St Joseph help the local priest conduct the services. There is a public footpath leading behind the church, but this is difficult to reach from the church itself. Instead, walk east along the main street back towards the bountiful fruit tree. Here Syerscote Lane takes us south for 400m before turning off south-east across the field.

Ahead we can glimpse the collection of farm buildings and hall which make up Thorpe Constantine, which stands on a rise with a number of quite obvious trees. Although this is not the target of the ley line, it is the visible pointer for our walk. Keeping the target in sight we follow the footpath south-east. A small brook is crossed via two footbridges, thereafter taking the right-hand footpath to cross Clifton Lane. Incidentally looking to your left there is a magnificent spire to be seen, instantly recognisable with its flying buttresses. This is the Church of St Andrew's at Clifton Campville, often referred to as the loveliest parish church in the county of Staffordshire.

Across the lane the path slowly climbs alongside the trees. Reaching Thorpe lane, turn right and head south. We are now over 700m from the original line of the track; from now we shall be closing this gap as we head for the next marker. This is a delightful walk of almost 2km along a quite lovely country lane, although beware of the cars here for some seem to think 60mph is an obligatory speed and not a limit.

Eventually we arrive at Seckington and its crossroads. This is the marker and not the motte and bailey we encounter in chapter eighteen. Standing on the obvious rise we can look back across the 4km to our starting point at Haunton. It is not easy to see, despite being more than 30m below us, yet when conditions are right it does give an idea of the

ABOVE: St Michael and St James's Church at Haunton in Staffordshire.

LEFT: St Andrew's, Clifton Campville.

route taken by our ancestors. While gazing back in one direction, take the trouble to look ahead. Again the visibility is not perfect, yet it does afford reasonable views of some of the sites and obstacles we are about to encounter. Not least of these are the four lanes of the M42, which we have heard on the breeze since reaching this high point of the crossroads.

Head straight across the crossroads and walk down the slope for 300m to turn left along Newton Lane. There are no turnings off this lane until we reach the junction on the outskirts of Newton Regis, where we take the road to the right and then 40m along left across the field. This footpath leads us underneath the motorway. To our left is the village of Austrey. Ignore the footpath heading there and carry straight on to join Warton Lane. Turn south along this lane, cross Bramcote Brook and just 80m along, at the field boundary on the right, we are back on the line of the ancient track once more.

Follow Warton Lane until reaching the corner at the Elms, turning left along Austrey Road, which becomes first Maypole Road and then Little Warton Road. A few houses along from the school and the junction with Barn End Road, there is a footpath. There can be no doubt where it is heading for ahead of us looms the prominent shape of Orton-on-the-Hill and its church dedicated to St Edith. During the spring and the early summer this path is clearly marked out by a yellow line across the land, easily seen from the hill.

It is a fairly flat walk from Warton until nearing the hill. There are a number of possible paths; we shall remain as close to the original track as it is possible to do. Therefore when we reach Warton Lane and turn right some 300m down this lane, there is a footpath heading south-east towards a crossroads of footpaths. Head straight between Hollis Farm and Moor Barns Farm buildings, over the summit of the hill and following the path of Green Lane. There are two paths running almost parallel to the south here; it is not the first but the second we should take, which we find having crossed the small brook.

Following the path south we meander alongside the brook and down to Benn Hill Farm, where we join Crow Lane, a minor road leading to Sheepy Road. Turn left and follow Ratcliffe Lane. As we cross the top of the small rise we catch sight of the fourteenth-century All Saints' Church, which stands alongside our next target, which we are unable to see at this point. Turn left at the junction and follow Pinwall Lane across the River Sence (courtesy of Ratcliffe Bridge) and then take the left fork in the road along Main Road and then right along Church Lane.

In a field behind the church is a moat, not a defensive feature for it is only 10m across and would not have been of any use as such. The term 'moat' is somewhat misleading, for today it is solely applied to a water-filled ditch around a castle or other defensive home. However, historically speaking it refers simply to a ditch which allowed water to collect there. As mentioned earlier the glistening of any light on water, even on the dullest of days, can be seen for a great distance. This marker is 10km from the crossroads at Seckington and could never have been the next marker point – it is simply too far away and there would have been little or no visibility between the two. Therefore there are missing markers here – nothing unusual, for there are many more missing on every ley than those we can find today.

From the moat look south-east along the ley. There is a small but obvious rise a kilometre away almost exactly on the line, just slightly to the left of the ley. However it is close enough to the path for us to be certain there was once a marker here: any pile of stones (or maybe even a standing stone) would have been very easy to see against the skyline.

Four hundred metres further on is a sharp angle in Atterton Lane; such a line is unusual for there are no natural features in the landscape to produce such a sharp bend. Normally we would expect to find other tracks, a stream, a field boundary, or even a political boundary. However, there are no such boundaries, either today or historically.

The only explanation is this was where another path met the Atterton Lane, most likely

The moat at Ratcliffe Culey, with All Saints' Church in the background.

the one we are following or a one that replaced it. There is no record of a lane on ancient maps, while any archaeological evidence disappeared under the ploughshare centuries ago. Atterton does not feature on this trackway, but we shall be passing close to this small farming community of just forty-six individuals (in 2000) very shortly.

Our route forces us to take a more easterly direction than the ley. From the church a short footpath crosses the field with the moat and we continue along this path to Ormes Lane. Turn left here and follow this north towards the Gate Inn, a pub which dates from at least the middle of the nineteenth century. At the dog-leg in Ormes Lane turn sharply right and follow the footpath east for 400m. Take the left path here to Ratcliffe House Lane. Follow this path to the house itself and then turn right along the path which follows the field boundaries to the aforementioned Atterton.

As we arrive at Atterton Lane, ahead of us along the footpath is Fenny Drayton and the church which stands out on the top of the hill here, dedicated to St Michael and All Angels. Coming across the field the houses are almost upon us when we can turn along the hedgerow and exit the field on to the A444 Atherstone Road opposite Fenn Lanes, known to have been a Roman road. Following the road south we arrive at a modern footpath on the right giving access to Hunters Lane. This point marks where we cross the ley once more.

From here we have a decision to make. Much of the earlier track is long buried beneath the streets of modern Nuneaton or affected so greatly we are unable to follow it for long across country. Most of the routes lead us around the north-east of the town via the Watling Street or south into Nuneaton by roads which avoid the railway.

Continue along the road south to the A5 Roman road and turn left. When we have travelled a kilometre along here we arrive at Mira Drive leading off to the left. This is not an official marker but does give a reference point to show where we are crossing the ley once more. We continue on to the island and turn right.

Walk south for 400m along Higham Lane and pause at the corner of Milby Drive to view the next marker point. Most unusually this is a farm, specifically Top Farm, just 200m west of here. It deserves its name for its stands on the crest of a small but noticeable rise. We could have reached it by taking a walk around a loop taking in Weddington, but the detour and the extra distance are not worthwhile for there is little to see which cannot be seen from this vantage point.

Turn east along Milby Drive and follow it around to the end where we turn left on to Pallett Drive and then the same to come to St Nicholas Park Drive. This road brings us to around below St Nicholas Park and to the A47 Hinckley Road where we turn left and then right at the island along the A4254 Eastboro Way. Just 500m along we reach the railway line: do not cross it here, but instead turn left alongside the embankment to where there is a tunnel to take us beneath it.

Once again we should pause, this time to look north to where three field boundaries meet at a point which, while not a marker in any actual sense, does show where the ley has come to. However, modern development has made the chance of any visibility along the line, in either direction, impossible. This is not the case when we pass beneath the railway line, for the region of our destination is visible to the south-east.

Although we are almost 3km away from the Church of St Bodolph's at Burton Hastings, it is quite evident in the distance. However, to get there we have to cross no less than five watercourses, the first of which we soon encounter as we follow the footpath east from the embankment. This small stream is Harrow Brook, just 400m away, followed by Sketchley Brook another 500m away and then the field boundary.

Here we come to another footpath where we turn right: 20m later we are turning left on to Hydes Lane, and then 20m along here, right. We are now heading south and, 400m along here, come to a small area of a few farm buildings on the left. Follow this path to the left and, where the path splits in two follow the right-hand one heading more directly toward the church at Burton Hastings.

We cross an unnamed brook on the kilometre walk across the fields, finally arriving at

Mill mound at Burton Hastings.

the River Anker. Crossing this river early on its 35km course north-west is not difficult; it is still a young river here, and we continue along the same heading to reach the bridge over the Ashby-de-la-Zouch Canal. Turn right along the tow path and, after the bend, look in the field to the west and you will see our final destination.

Despite it having been empty for several centuries, the mill mound is still quite obvious here. It stands alongside Mill Lane, itself leading to a former watermill. The mound was not a part of the workings of the watermill, nor was it a mound for windmills, which were not seen in this country until a much later date. The name is likely misleading, although it is accurate. The mound is thought to have been created to support a marker of some description, most likely one of stone or stones, but possibly where a tree stood out. It does not refer to the mound being something to do with the mill; instead, it is said to be 'by the mill' or even Mill Lane. Clearly this was not the original name, for the marker would have been here centuries before the mill.

Standing here we can look back in the general direction of the ley but, even though we are aware of the mark points, are not really able to see much in the modern landscape. The topography of the land would have changed little, if at all, so this tells us that the original markers would have been quite clear in the landscape. I left the site reflecting on just what form these markers would have taken as I made my way back along the Ashby Canal to Stoke Golding, where I hired a small craft for a few days' relaxation on a canal which (thankfully) had no locks for my tired limbs to negotiate.

CHAPTER SEVEN

MALVERN TO BRAILES

This is the chosen route of several from the British Camp on the Malvern Hills. Whilst this may not be nearly as grand as the stone circles at Avebury or Stonehenge, or as prominent as the mountains of the Lake or Peak Districts, from a cultural perspective it is as important.

Although the Malverns are as well known for its spring water as for anything else, to climb here and examine the toposcope which points out the direction and the distance of over seventy places which can be seen from this vantage point is an indication of its importance. In fact, this large hill fort could comfortably house 2,000 individuals. Furthermore it was, and still is, a major hub for ancient trackways stretching across not only the Midlands, but England and Wales. In this chapter we are concerned with following a path almost directly east, across Worcestershire to Warwickshire and towards the Cotswolds.

It is almost 20km to the next known marker on Bredon Hill. This is a much longer step than we would normally find between points, but this does not make the ley any less certain. The markers, which would doubtless have existed, have simply been lost through one (or more) of a great number of reasons which can be summed up as progress.

The route taken by the earliest traders between the British Camp at Malvern and Bredon Hill would have originally been a direct one. The modern landscape makes it difficult to see how they traversed some of the obstacles, yet we shall be following the original path as closely as possible. From the British Camp the simplest route would be to follow the A4104 on foot until we have crossed the River Severn. However, this has certainly not been in existence since antiquity, thus cannot be anything to do with the ley. Hence I decided to take the public footpaths whenever possible.

This is how we come to be heading south along the ridge of the Malverns following the modern route known as the Worcestershire Way Link. Follow the contour through woodland below the summit, turning east around Hangman's Hill and descending in a north-easterly direction through Shadybank Common. The views to Bredon Hill are uninterrupted, although the ley is not apparent as we are still some way south of the alignment; we can also clearly see our target of the village of Welland.

It would have been fitting if we could have described the present route to take by giving contemporary landmarks. The original markers stood out, literally, when all that could be seen was the natural canopy of woodland – anything artificial stood out clearly. Today there is so much diversity; things which are so familiar we tend to ignore, and the sighting points have to be very obvious.

Ask directions today and you will hear a list of road names and/or designations. Alternatively large department stores or supermarkets and traffic lights are easily noticed and well remembered. I recall my father telling of when he was a young man, a time of much less traffic and when there was a pub seemingly on every corner, and recognition points were restricted to public houses and churches. So we are forced to keep our eyes on the map and on the ground, as so few of the landmarks are actually visible today except when we are so close as to offer no directional clues of note.

Hence our journey east continues and just below the fittingly named Underhills Farm we swing east, dropping down a slope until we reach Hancocks Lane. We are now on the modern footpath known as the Worcestershire Way Link, a well-marked path which we shall follow for 4km south of Welland along a route which parallels the ancient one. Undoubtedly this village once had a marker, which would have been near the crossroads. It would not have been at the place of worship, but alongside the green north of the public house known as the Pheasant Inn.

It is not hard to see on a map how Marlbank Road once came directly to the crossroads. Yet modern planners have provided a gentle loop to ease traffic problems, little realising that this would have been the earliest track marked out through here, well before the village or its name even existed. While we could follow the road, the public footpath offers a quieter journey and a less cluttered view of the landscape, and we shall be walking the road before long.

It is approximately 4km along the footpath, the yellow markers pointing the way as clearly as any. With little deviation we cross Gloucester Road and the little-used track to Hurst Farm, the land gently rolling downwards and offering not much of a challenge as it drops down to the distant river.

Ahead of us, and slightly to the north, lies Welland Lodge and, to the south, Welland Court. What little track remains lies between, and marks where we leave the Worcestershire Way Link and take the footpath through Lockeridge Farm to join the A4104 Welland Road at Duckswich.

Follow the road for just over a kilometre and we come to Tunnel Hill. This is not a particularly old place name; it refers to the railway line which runs through here. There is a scattering of housing here, besides the farms. Yet, once again, we can be fairly certain that a marker once stood here: the hill would have been a favoured sighting point. What form this marker took is unknown, yet it seems likely to have been a pile of stones or similar, something which would have been visible to the naked eye from a reasonable distance.

The ley crosses this hamlet at a point exactly where the road known as Packers Hill leads off Greenfields. Although these names will have been taken from existing fields, they cannot be considered as being related to the ley in any way. The next time our path crosses the ancient route may well be by a marker.

Further along the A4104, where the name changes from Tunnel Hill to Old Street, there is a loop of an old country lane. This junction marks where the ley crosses, though it does not align with either end. The trunk road bends to the left, for very good reasons, for ahead of us is a major obstacle, the longest river in the land – the Severn.

Just how the ancients crossed this major river here is unproven. It is likely there was a ferry or bridge, as any suggestion of a ford seems quite impractical. South of the ley the first bridge carries the M50 west. There was once a railway bridge a kilometre south of

The modern bridge next to the fording point at Shipston-on-Stow.

the ley, the same line which gave Tunnel Hill its name. However, the track was lifted years ago and the bridge is long gone, which is a shame for it would have made an excellent footbridge. Our only feasible means of crossing the river today is travelling north through Upton-on-Severn to the Upton Bridge. Follow Old Street, Hight Street and Church Street to the bridge and cross the river.

Immediately across the other side a path runs along the right bank, crossing the bridge at the mouth of the marina and along the bank until it reaches Ryall and the road known as Ryall Meadow. This only gives us 75m of path before we turn off south and, after 600m, turn sharply left at the waterworks. This path takes us parallel with the ley and less than 100m south of it. Shortly we cross the A30 and then down into the very small hamlet of Naunton.

Making our way through Fowler's Copy Farm, we continue west up an increasingly noticeable rise. The ley line to the north passes near Hill Croome, a small place which reaches the staggering height of 29m above sea level at the oddly named Wooshill. Whilst this hardly qualifies as a 'hill' in the traditional sense, it clearly stands out above the surrounding land and would doubtless have provided the perfect setting for another marker. One kilometre along we arrive at Upper Strensham (which is better known for giving its name to the motorway services on the M5).

We have managed to cross one obstacle, the Severn, by diverting to take the only bridge available to us on foot. We are now faced by three others in quick succession, only one of which would have been in the path of our ancestors, the River Avon. Ironically, the M5, Avon and railway line do not force us to deviate greatly – it is the sewage farm on the right bank which proves a major problem. There are two choices, south to the village of Bredon, or north to Eckington. The latter is somewhat closer to the ley, affords better views, and is undoubtedly a far more pleasant walk.

Thus we emerge into Upper Strensham along Twyning Road which, whilst it may not be particularly straight, does take us along a gentle hill to Mill Lane and the bridge across the motorway. The sight (and sound) from this busy artery to the south-west leave us in no doubt as to the direction to take.

Mill Lane continues on to, and then north, through the sewage farm which makes it passable on this left bank. At Rockridge Farm, take the path left towards the river and cross to the island in the centre. This is an important point because we are standing on the ley and must have been where the Avon was crossed. Again it seems likely to have been forded: it is easy to imagine stakes driven into the bed of the stream supporting planks forming a walkway to allow passage. No archaeological evidence has been found here, yet it was certainly not beyond their technology, for to the south across the marshes which covered much of Somerset such constructions have been traced for miles.

Follow the footpath upstream, across the weir and then via the lock to the opposite bank where we continue to follow Mill Lane away from the river towards Eckington. Mill Lane here becomes Station Road, where we take the next left along Boon Street, and from there go right along Drakes Bridge Road. We follow this road through Eckington, noting it becomes New Road and then Nafford Road until, 600m from the bridge, we turn left along Upper Edge. This street bends left and then right when it becomes Oatsley Lane, which is where we leave Eckington and head east along the footpath from Upper End Farm.

Ahead of us rises Bredon Hill, the gradient becoming increasingly more difficult after crossing Comberton Road. At Woollas Hall Farm the path turns more south and up to the ridge, where we turn left and enjoy an easier climb to the tower at Bredon and meet up once again with the ley.

A.E. Houseman immortalised Bredon Hill in his most famous work, *A Shropshire Lad*. The name Bredon Hill has three elements from three ancient languages: Celtic *bre*, Old English *dun* and Middle English *hyll* all mean exactly the same. Thus the literal meaning of this place name is 'hill, hill, hill'.

Having climbed it I can attest there can be no doubt that this is a hill, although it is seems it was apparently not sufficiently high for one John Parsons of Kemerton. During the latter half of the eighteenth century, Parsons was squire of Kemerton and also served as the Member of Parliament for this place. He paid for the building of a summer house at the top of the hill. This folly is 11.9m in height and stands at the top of Bredon Hill's 293m. Using the metric system of measurement this has little significance. However, when this was built the imperial system was in use and the tower of 39ft added to the 961ft of the hill making it exactly 1,000ft.

Alongside Parsons Folly is Bambury Stone, a natural outcrop of the conglomerate rock from which the hill was formed. It is said to resemble an elephant. In order to see this form, one has to stand behind and to the left. Residents near the hill speak of the treasure hidden beneath the elephant; the creature allegedly leaves its vantage point when it hears the clock at Pershore Abbey strike midnight and goes down to the Avon to drink (which forms the hill). Others believe this stone was used as an altar by the Druids in their ceremonies. I was told it was considered good luck to kiss the stone on Good Friday.

Other standing stones here, a little below the summit, are known as the King and Queen Stones. In times past the sick were passed between the stones in an attempt to heal them. These likely also formed part of the ceremonial backdrop along with the Bambury Stone. All these stones are still considered to be a source of great power by those with an interest in witchcraft and the occult.

Designated a Special Area of Conservation, the hill provides habitats for rare invertebrates including the violet click beetle (*Limoniscus violaceus*). This beetle has always been extremely

Is this an elephant? The Bambury Stone, Bredon Hill.

rare to our shores, only ever seen here, at nearby Dixton Wood and in Windsor Forest (where it was first identified as late as 1937). Once found throughout much of the land, the population of these creatures has shrunk (along with the regions of ancient woodland upon which it relies for its existence). Along with several other endangered species listed in the Red Data Book, the beetle can only exist on the decaying timbers of ancient trees. Several organisations work together to maintain the ancient woodland, the grassland and the scrub and preserve the habitat.

Continue to follow the ridge for about a kilometre. Here the path splits – take the first path to the south along the edge of the woodland, coming to the Wychavon Way. Follow the left path and descend through the wood, skirting Fiddler's Knap until you come to Kersoe Road. We have just circled the next marker, the ancient site of Elmley Castle above us which, when I walked it, was out of bounds (although hopefully this will not continue to be the case for too long).

While a castle may not normally be considered a typical marker, the reasons for the sighting of the eleventh-century Norman stronghold would have applied in earlier times too. The village of Elmley Castle took its name from Old English for 'the woodland clearing among the elm trees'; the additional 'castle' was not seen until the early fourteenth century. Today we find the name, the occasional stone and obvious earthworks as the only evidence that anything ever stood here.

Elmley Castle was reputedly built by Robert le Despenser, and was later home to the Beauchamp family. It passed, through a female line, to the Savage family – one of whom, Sir John Savage, is depicted receiving Queen Elizabeth I to the village on 20 August 1575 on the sign outside the local Queen's Head Hotel. Standing at the highest point in the village, the original building was a ruin by 1316 and was rebuilt later that century. Two hundred years later the building was uninhabitable, and the stones were gradually re-used elsewhere.

All this building work has destroyed any chance of finding much evidence of earlier habitation. However, there can be little doubt that such habitation existed – and had done for a very long time.

We have emerged near Ballard's Farm. Follow the road east through the tiny hamlet of Kersoe, along Station Road, crossing the old dismantled railway line, then right around the loop of Bank Cottages and around to find the next marker, the crossroads at Hinton Cross and the A46 Cheltenham Road.

It is easy to see this as the junction point of three roads. In modern terms this is evidently the case, albeit modern safety concerns have changed the route a little. Historically, however, it would have been seen as the place where five routes converged at a single spot. Furthermore, this place would have been marked by a cross, hence the name.

There are no indications, either physical or documented, that this was ever a meeting place. However there seems to be little doubt this was the purpose, for the name of this place is virtual confirmation alone. This would not have been where the meeting took place but where the delegates assembled at a nearby hall, such as a forerunner of the manor house here which we have just passed.

We must head south-west along the Hinton Road. There is a footpath some 200m along here leading off to Wickhamford, yet this takes us quite some distance away, so we will continue on to Mount Pleasant Cottages and take this footpath north to Murcot and along Murcot Turn. When we reach the footpath opposite Tally-ho Cottages we cross the ley and continue on to the Evesham Road on the crest of the ridge. Turn right at the junction and after 200m turn left to pass Gallipot Farm House. Shortly after the path forks, take the right-hand path and follow your nose towards Willersley. Saintbury Cross should not be considered in any way an original marker; it is only the positioning which is original. Indeed what we see today, a Maltese cross and a sundial, was added in 1848, although the lower features date from the fifteenth century.

Arriving at the crossroads north of the village, head north-east along Weston Lane and we come to the next marker point, the cross north of the hamlet. A little more than 200m east along the ley is an earthwork. This ancient double rampart and ditch is very small for such a construction, the interior only 50m in diameter. Today trees cut through the centre and the southern half has disappeared completely, ploughed out centuries ago.

Our path continues along Weston Lane to the junction where we turn left along Buckle Street, then right along Parson's Lane, and right again down Chapel Lane. Fifty metres before the end there is a footpath leading south: take it and then the east path away from the site of the former manor house. Ascending the increasing gradient along this path we enter The Lynches Wood, emerging on the summit of Dover's Hill.

Undoubtedly a marker of some description once stood here, for this is where the ley runs across Dover's Hill near to Chipping Campden. It has been thought that a turf maze was once constructed in a natural amphitheatre on Dover's Hill. Confined to England, Germany and Denmark, turf mazes were later versions of the very ancient stone puzzles. There is a major problem when attempting to date turf mazes, as the very fact that they have to be re-cut regularly to maintain a clear design means the archaeology is constantly swept clean.

The purpose of the mazes is less than clear. Since medieval times they were used by penitents who would follow the paths on their hands and knees, stopping at certain points for prayer. In recent times several of the sites have been used for annual festivities, particularly in spring around Easter, Whitsuntide and May Day. However, few can be more unique than the Cotswold Games, also known as Dover's Olympick Games.

Since 1610 Chipping Campden has been home to unusual rural games. Held every year on the Friday evening of what is now known as Spring Bank Holiday week and formerly

Saintbury Cross.

The toposcope on Dover's Hill, looking 25m to the Malverns beyond the trees.

Whitsuntide, the events are variations on the usual sporting theme – with a few exceptions. For instance, there is the ignoble art of shin-kicking which, despite how it appears, should be seen as a test of maintaining one's balance rather than one of painful endurance. Stuffing hay down the legs of the trousers is allowed, but only for the participants. At the conclusion of the events a large bonfire is lit and a firework display entertains the assembly. Afterwards there is a procession by torchlight back to the village square and dancing to live music.

The following day fancy dress is worn by locals who trail behind a decorated float pulled by Morris Men and on which sits the Scuttlebrook May Queen (accompanied by her four specially chosen attendants and a page boy). Prizes are later awarded in a variety of categories, with organised dancing displays and a final procession on to the fairground.

While the ley heads off to the east to its terminus at Brailes Hill, we must take an alternative route. Climb to Bold Gap and then take the left-hand path down to Kingcomb Lane; turning left, follow this to the junction with Aston Road, which is the point where the ley grazes our track once again. It does not seem likely this was ever a marker. However, it does help us to mention any potential sighting point. While visibility may never be possible, changing seasons, lighting and weather conditions can make a great difference and what was unseen one day may be obvious at another time. Thus it is always worthwhile taking any opportunity to look along a ley, the only reason we ventured on this detour.

Turn south along Aston Road towards Chipping Campden. On reaching Cidermill Lane turn left along it and continue forward along Station Road, following it to the left for a kilometre or so. This road will take us across the railway line at Battle Bridge, and from there up a gentle slope until we come to Campden Road.

For the vast majority of the remainder of our journey we will be staying on the roads. Not only do they provide a more direct route, but also if we were to attempt to take footpaths from here the length of our meandering would be more than challenging.

However, the roads do have the drawback of being fairly straight and thus rarely cross the ley.

Here we take Campden Road to Ebrington; at the junction turn right along Hidcote Road, then left along Campden Road. Here it would interest the historian to take a look at the site of the former Roman villa at the Grove opposite Nash's Lane. Not much is visible above ground: what remains has been left beneath the soil by archaeologists. Yet it is certainly worthwhile taking the time to look around before continuing on towards Shipston-on-Stour. It may be better to continue south along Hidcote Road past the church where, 120m along here, a footpath leading west crosses the Roman site and shortly afterwards meets up with the road once more.

Follow this lane east up the slope to Charingworth and on up to Goose Hill. Here we are as far from the ley as we are going to get. The original track is 400m north of us crossing through the southern edge of the lost medieval village of Compton Scorpion, little of which remains today save for the name (which has been taken by the manor house).

Now the road bends northwards and continues to undulate over a dismantled railway line and the Fosse Way, reaching the ley again at Mount Farm, shortly before we enter Shipston-on-Stour. The ley crossing the Fosse Way has no potential marker today, not even a clue in the modern field boundaries. From this we can see the ley line predates the road. Furthermore, it was likely to have fallen out of use by the time the Roman road was constructed.

Our route takes us by the quickest route through Shipston and across the Stour. Campden Road becomes West Street, and then Mill Street across the river. The ley crosses the river 50m south of the bridge and then skirts the southern slopes of Borough Hill, where there would undoubtedly once have been a sighting point 20m below the summit. Between these two points it touches around the junction of Mill Street and Fell Mill Lane

Castle Hill at Brailes.

(this is not a marker, however, but is just a reference point).

There are no footpaths along here to help us along the trackway, hence we continue east along the lane known as Fant Hill passing north of Brailes Hill. North of the villages take the lane to the left known as Castle Hill and then the footpath heading directly to the ancient site of the earthwork which gives the hill its name.

Reaching Brailes the trackway hits Castle Hill. This place affords commanding views over the villages of Upper and Lower Brailes. A very worn and much altered central oval flat top, measuring between 10m and 30m in diameter and at around 150m above sea level, stands above a clear earthwork covering over one hectare. Although worn, it is still possible to see the earth banks which would encircle the site, though they have been subjected to weathering and have eroded away in the east. This was a motte and bailey, the site being abandoned shortly after its construction in the early twelfth century. The day I went it looked quite lovely, the last overnight snow shower of the winter still to be thawed by the rising sun, while the coming of spring was all around in the shape of the flowering broom.

Intervisibility along the ley is not possible, the distances and topography making it impractical. This was a direct path of 50km and we walked at least seventy (and probably more) over a period of three days, although it could probably be done in two without pausing to take in the views. However, to ignore the beauty of this walk, despite the distance walked along country lanes, would be a pity.

Not only was this the longest trek, but also it was among the most memorable.

CHAPTER EIGHT

BURIAL PATH AT FECKENHAM

Not all ancient trackways were trade routes. In times when not every hamlet had its own churchyard, or even its own church, it was necessary to take the deceased to the nearest graveyard for burial. Today a few of these funeral tracks are still found, one of the most obvious being this trackway to Feckenham in Worcestershire.

Whilst it is true to say that any ancient pathways will have pre-dated Christianity by several centuries, places of pagan worship and burial mounds are found on the route. As England was converted to Christianity it made sense to erect the new churches on the sacred sites where worshippers already gathered. At a stroke the earlier religions had been replaced, yet the venue remained – and it was one the congregation were used to. It is for this very reason that so many churches are found on leys, even though there was a great deal of time between the marking of the ley and the advent of Christianity.

The two are connected, albeit not directly, but not because of any religious reasons. In fact, even the earlier pagan religions were sited here well after the track had been marked out – not just by a few years, or even a few decades, but probably 1,000 or more years.

Two adjacent hamlets south-west of Redditch had no means of burying their dead. Thus Cruise Hill and Ham Green were forced to use the closest ground available, which just happened to be two miles south at Feckenham. As we follow this comparatively short two-mile pathway there are unusual and also obvious reminders to be found. There is only one way to follow this trackway, in the same direction taken by funeral processions for so many years, directly south.

From Cruise Hill the pathway predictably descends. Behind us the remains of a chapel stands alongside a road with a modern road sign displaying an ancient and telling name: Burial Lane. Here the lane is enclosed on both sides by woodland. This is what remains of the ancient Feckenham Forest, which once covered a large part of Worcestershire. In 1608, when it had shrunk to under 9,000 hectares and become little more than a park, the forest was released by the Crown and became common land.

Following the track today, we see that it has sadly been influenced by modern field boundaries. The second path from Ham Green has been so distorted it is now a tortuous winding track which has hidden the original route completely. Yet both show the obvious

A modern sign showing an ancient path.

destination of St John the Baptist Church almost with every step, particularly during the winter months when the leaves are on the path and not on the trees.

This is, for the most part, a refreshingly broad path. As evidenced by the horseshoe marks heading both up and down here, this is a much-used bridle path. Ahead of us, slightly to the left, is Dunstall Court. This Elizabethan house was rebuilt in 1844 and is probably the major reason for the field boundary changes which had been standing for centuries before the house was ever considered.

Approximately a kilometre before reaching our destination the footpath takes us on a detour looping westward. This takes us over the footbridge over Swans Brook and around the pond serving the building which once stood at this end of Mill Lane. Three other paths converge at this point, where the mill race is still quite clearly seen, but the lane we require is obvious. Heading south-west, take Mill Lane toward the church where, 400m along, we pass between an ancient cross to the north and an earthwork to the south. This latter feature lies directly in the path of the ley.

While there has been much speculation and archaeological work done on both the cross and the earthwork, very little has been found to suggest the origins of either. It seems likely the cross has nothing to do with the ley, although it may well have replaced earlier versions. The earthwork poses more of a problem, for the little evidence uncovered is inconclusive. It is likely that the place was in use, for whatever reason, for such a short period that there was no time for evidence to build up.

What is clear is that the village cricket ground is among the best kept. Care seems to have been lavished on every blade of grass and it provides the perfect area for this most English of games. The day I walked here cricket was still several weeks away, yet work on preparing for the coming season had been carried on all winter.

If we were to extend this ley for a further 100m it would come to the B4090, known to be the Roman road linking Ryknild Street at Alcester with Droitwich. It is still known as the Salt Way and would have been known as such well before the arrival of the Romans. We shall examine this route in chapter 23.

The well-worn ancient burial track.

CHAPTER NINE

MAY HILL LEY

This ley is always cited as running the opposite way, although of course these ancient trackways had no real right or wrong way any more than any trunk road does today. It is referred to as the May Hill Ley and for the author this made it the obvious starting point.

The day this ley was walked started off in reasonable weather, yet the forecast for later in the day was less than promising. To walk to the top of this hill some 295m (971ft) above sea level and not be able to enjoy the view was foolhardy. This decision was quite clearly the correct one for the memorable views of the Malverns to the north, the Forest of Dean to the south, the city of Gloucester and the Severn in the east, and even the Black Mountains of Wales.

Other than the views there is more here to hold the interest. As the hill is approached there is a very obvious group of trees on the summit. These are not natural, although there is no way to know this by the appearance: they were planted to mark the Golden Jubilee of Queen Victoria and have become a well-known landmark. Smaller trees grow here, planted to mark the Silver Jubilee of Queen Elizabeth II. Prior to these plantings, the summit was known to be bare, though an earlier map does show pines grew here previously.

For years the summit has been the site of May Day celebrations, which has been said to be why the name was changed from the earlier Yartleton Hill. While the etymology may be correct, it is more likely the same hill was known by two different names from those who lived (for example) on the lower slopes on opposite sides. Thus there was never any official name change: one name simply fell out of use. Incidentally, the road passing nearby here still bears the name of Yartleton Lane.

From the start point follow the Gloucestershire Way south-west through May Hill village and Gander's Green. The path climbs Bright's Hill where, as we cross the summit, we can see the spire of the Church of St John the Baptist at Huntley. While this is not a ley marker, it is a good target point for us to aim for and provides us with a place to leave the Gloucestershire Way and head parallel to the A40 toward Huntley itself.

Emerging at Newent Lane, turn right and then left to follow the trunk road to Solomons Tump Road immediately after the golf course. Opposite this delightfully named road is a footpath skirting the wood: follow it and rejoin the Gloucestershire Way heading east. Continue and cross Chapel Lane, and 300m further on turn south.

Looking back having just crossed the Severn, May Hill is visible between the trees.

Having crossed a footbridge and passed the cheesemaker's premises, the path veers towards the south-east, passing east of Ley Court Wood and under the railway line. Shortly we reach the intriguingly named Ley Road; this has nothing to do with ley lines, strangely, for it was so named many years before Alfred Watkins gave trackways this name in his book *The Old Straight Track* in the early part of the twentieth century. Follow the lane for 100m then turn left along the footpath across the footbridge to skirt Denny Hill, cross Oakle Street and arrive at the A48 and the River Severn at what is known as Placket Pool.

Once there must have been a crossing here, the ley cutting across from Duni Farm to Elmore Back Farm. I had arranged to be collected and the car provided a welcome rest for my feet as it took a most circuitous route along the A40 and A38 around to be dropped at Weir Farm east of Farley's End. Here, where the lane leads off Elmore Road, we are standing on the ley once more.

Following the lane south from here we soon see the next obstacle on our route, this time a man-made watercourse, the Gloucester and Sharpness Canal. We have taken this road for a reason, for it, along with Sellars Bridge, provides the perfect artery in a region which is short on footpaths. Ahead of us is the southern edge of the city of Gloucester, the A38 trunk road, the even busier M5 motorway, and the railway line heading down towards Bristol and the South West.

Having crossed the canal we come to a traffic island: straight across is School Lane, which leads us to another island where we take a right along Field Court Drive. This cuts through a residential district to a third traffic island, continuing across as Naas Lane and crossing the A38. By the time we leave the tarmac once more and rejoin the paths marked out across the countryside we have travelled almost 3km.

We left the motorway behind us 500m back and the road bends sharply to the right. Ahead of us is a footpath and we shall take it across the footbridge, and parallel with Naas Lane, until reaching the lane again we turn left and follow it north to the junction – where we turn right and east. Six hundred metres along here a footpath enables us to cut off the corner and take a shortcut to the A4173. Cross the road and take the footpath little more than 30m to the north which heads east and then south-east.

We have a tough climb ahead of us to the ridge known as Huddinknoll Hill. However, it is worth it, for the views along the ley from the top are quite excellent, particularly back along the ancient trackway across the Severn Valley. At the top we are 200m above sea level; the crossing point at the Severn was a little under 10m above high tide at the coast.

The footpath to take is that heading towards Painswick to the south-east, now clearly visible and easy to follow along the pathways leading down the slopes in the direction of the village. By the time we reach Edge Lane we are climbing again, but up a much less strenuous gradient. The picturesque village of Painswick soon appears and thoughts turn to the prospect of finding our next ley marker.

Approaching Painswick it soon becomes obvious that our target is the church, the tower standing out against the background. While the majority of the church is fifteenth century, the tower itself is Norman with Saxon influences. When close enough scrutinise the tower, the marks left by cannonballs during the bombardment of the English Civil War are still visible. Parliamentarians had taken refuge in the church; however, the siege was brief and decisive. The combination of cannon and the burning brands of the Royalist troops forced them out into the open.

Entering the churchyard of St Mary's we pass through the lych-gate, a fairly recent construction from much older timbers taken from the belfry. Such seemingly grand covered entrances were once functional, for this was where the funeral procession would pause with the coffin sheltered from any inclement weather awaiting the priest who was to conduct the ceremony.

Also seen in the entry are some unusual spectacle stocks, so called for the obvious resemblance to the optical aids. Through the gate the mourners would have entered a churchyard with many splendid tombs paid for by the beneficiaries of wealthy wool merchants. However, the eye is soon caught by the yew trees.

Most old churchyards have yew trees. These large, slow-growing trees were often planted near to churches. Hallowed ground is protected against the plough, but not always grazing animals. However, the leaves of the yew contain poison which makes them unpalatable and this is why these trees, which can be easily over 1,000 years old, are found near churches.

In St Mary's there are many more yews than are ever seen in most churchyards, even the largest. The number of yews here has spawned two legends. To attempt to count them is, on the one hand, considered foolhardy, for no matter how many times they are counted a different total will be arrived at each time. Yet the second story tells us there are just ninety-nine trees, no more and no less. It is said that if just one more tree is planted the Devil will cause it to shrivel and die.

The most famous Painswick pastime is often associated with the yews, but has no connection with them. It occurs every year on the first Sunday following the 19 September and is known as the Clipping Ceremony. It is then that the children of the parish gather around inside the church to sing hymns while carrying locally grown flowers.

Leaving Painswick behind we head up the hill to Bull's Cross. From the church walk along Vicarage Street, turn right on to Friday Street and continue on to pass the ancient well site on Tibbiwell Lane. Carrying on, we walk up the lower slopes of Down Hill along Greenhouse Lane and Yokehouse Lane to Slad Lane and Bull's Cross.

Here is an old mounting block and milestone, quite possibly still in the same position as the earliest markers. There have been rumours of sightings of a phantom coach and horses charging across the high ground here, but nobody I spoke to had ever heard anything specific other than the rumours. It is generally believed that ghostly sightings are relevant

Painswick's lovely church, with its well-manicured yew trees.

to earlier events in this world. However, it seems highly improbable that a coach and horses could have ever run across such soft ground as is found here. Therefore the story is probably little more than legend, most likely having migrated from a reported sighting elsewhere.

Five hundred metres further along the ley crosses very close to the summit of the 200m high Down Hill, which would have made the perfect site for a marker although none exists today. We are unable to reach the summit, so we take the footpath known as Wysis Way south along Slad Road before heading across Down Hill and up on to the plateau via Trillgate Farm, Snow's Farm and Driftcombe Farm along the same footpath.

Here we find our next marker in a place name – Wittantree. This requires a little explanation, for otherwise there appears to be nothing here. Nearby is the village of Bisley, which gave its name to the hundred of Bisley Court. A hundred was an administrative sub-division of a county. How it got its name is a point of contention, for there are several possibilities: the most popular explanation is it refers to a region which was sufficient to provide a livelihood for 100 men-at-arms and their families. In the region of England once under Scandinavian influence, the term 'wapentake' is often used instead.

The Bisley Court hundred comprised seven parishes, none of which were known as Wittantree – so why the name? From the seventh to the eleventh centuries the local affairs of Saxon England were dealt with by the Witenagemot. This is comprised of two Old English words, *witan*, 'wise man' or 'counsellor', and *gemot*, 'assembly'. The term is often abbreviated to simply Witan, yet this should really only be applied to the individual members of the court.

It is known that the meeting place for Bisley Cross hundred was at the Stancombe crossroads north-west of Bisley on the road between Painswick and Cirencester. By the seventeenth century the local meetings were held in a building next to Bisley churchyard and, while the date of the last meeting is unrecorded, were certainly still held until at least 1740.

It is tempting to suggest the tree spoken of in the name was where the Witan originally met. However the more likely explanation is it marked the point on the trackway where the representatives should leave the ancient path and head for the actual meeting place nearby. There can be no doubt the marker was a tree. Furthermore, it would have been a prominent tree and probably already an ancient one when it became a marker.

The footpath continues on south-east to cross Calf Way, leading on to Cheltenham Road and Manor Street, before turning left along Van Der Breen Street. This lane leads to a footpath which we follow for 800m, down the slope and then turning right almost to double back up the slope. Eventually we come to Hayhedge Lane where, opposite the scrubland known as Battlescombe, is the last marker.

Hidden away alongside a field known as Giant's Grave is the final marker on this trackway. The site, known as Giant's Stone long barrow, has suffered much over the years and little is left today. Indeed, it was only with the help of copies of old maps that I was even able to find the present site. Also, not all of those showed the ancient burial mound, so it must have been in a very bad state for some considerable time.

Today the only remaining feature is a single stone. Certainly it is still in its original site, although if any of the other stones are still here is unknown, for there is a great deal of vegetation growing here, and the debris from several growing seasons is evident.

This walk would have been a little over 26km had we been able to walk it in its original straight line. Having been almost at sea level when crossing the Severn, we reach an altitude of almost 300m with a great deal of undulation in between. We have seen some of the most ancient of markers and managed to avoid modern society's express routes.

This walk affords some good views over the Vale of Gloucester and ahead to the Cotswolds, which will be walked elsewhere in this book.

CHAPTER TEN

SAINTBURY LEY

This is a ley which has been known for some time, though not the longest of paths, running just 6km from its starting point in a roughly southerly direction. Of course this does not mean the ley may not have been longer – there is simply no extant evidence to suggest further markers.

As discussed in the Malvern to Brailes ley (chapter seven), the crossroads may be a marker itself, but the cross here is in no way original: indeed, the base is no earlier than the fifteenth century, while the Maltese cross and sundial are documented as being added in 1848.

The line from here to the church was known as a funeral path. The procession would gather at the cross prior to making the ceremonial final journey to the church for burial. Clearly the funeral path could not have existed before the church. However, the procession may well have travelled from here to the site of the church when it was still a pagan site, although there is currently no archaeological evidence to prove this. Or the goal may have been another pagan cemetery further along the route, although this would seem to be a little too far to be practical.

From the crossroads follow the path south uphill towards the church. St Nicholas' Church is built on the side of the hill above Saintbury. The views from the church over the Vale of Evesham are worth lingering over, especially when the weather is not impairing vision too much.

The church is something of an oddity, for it has features from several quite diverse eras. Most of the church is Norman, with later enhancements including a Queen Anne vaulted roof. However, there was an earlier Saxon church on the same site, a part of which has been preserved in the south wall above a sealed doorway. Clearly the Normans felt it worthwhile keeping the mass dial (an early sundial). The impressive spire not only looks attractive but sounds good too as it houses six bells.

Yet surely the most surprising find here is the image of Sheila-na-gig on the south wall. Depicted as a female demon, this goddess of fertility was one of the highest ranking figures in British Celtic mythology. This is the strongest evidence that this place has been a site of worship for some time. To construct a church on the side of a hill would not be the first choice – but if the church was built here to replace the place of worship of the earlier pagan religion, it replaces the site and wipes clear the religion at a stroke. This is the main reason why churches are found on ley lines. This raises a question: having built upon the earlier pagan site, why would symbolism from that religion be incorporated into the masonry of the new building?

From the church, take the footpath south up the hill, turning left along Campden Lane and them immediately right along Buckle Street and passing between the former workings and the modern golf club.

The hill is properly known as Willersley Hill and it is up its slope that the path now leads us to the very summit and the next marker. Here is a Bronze-Age round barrow which has suffered greatly from the plough in earlier times. Today this 7m diameter barrow stands under a metre proud of the surrounding countryside and takes a little searching to find it. Excavated in 1935, archaeologists discovered there were earthworks surrounding the site. Today the locals know the place as Castle Bank, although whether this is an ancient name not recorded on any known maps or a modern creation is uncertain.

As we move on we find a Neolithic long barrow shortly afterwards, standing amid a twenty-five hectare Iron-Age fort. Clearly the fort, which can date from no earlier than 2500 BC, was constructed up to 1,000 years after the barrow and yet at no stage interferes with it. Today the area forms a part of the Broadway Golf Club. Landscaping has smoothed out much of the site today, but the excavation of 1884 revealed large stones presumed by archaeologists to be part of a collapsed chamber. The plough had also disturbed the site years before and, while ox and human bones were recovered, as they were not *in situ* it was virtually impossible to gather any information from them.

Approximately 600m from Campden Lane, turn right on to the Cotswold Way heading up towards Broadway Tower to take advantage of the views from up here. Approaching Beacon Tower on Broadway Hill we cross a Saxon cemetery. This is not a Christian but a pagan site, as evidenced by the mis-aligned burials. This is not considered to be a marker for a number of reasons: firstly, there is a lack of any further evidence; secondly, Saxon sites are rather late to be considered true markers, although it is possible that there was a marker here which has been erased by either Saxon work or the construction of the tower.

The tower was built in the 1790s by Lady Coventry and is also known as Broadway Tower or Fish Inn Tower. It was once home to William Morris, founder of the Arts and Crafts Movement. Today it is the most famous landmark around here, the high point of a popular country park. The view from the tower is splendid, and purportedly gives the naked eye views over no less than fourteen different counties.

From the tower, leave the Cotswold Way and follow the footpath south, dog-legging east to link up again with Buckle Street. Follow this street along the side of the woodland and then, 700m from the tower, turn sharp left to the terminus at Seven Wells Farm.

Straight ahead along the ley is Seven Wells Farm. Normally farms are avoided as potential markers for, by their very nature, they cover a comparatively large area and true markers are virtually pinpoints. However, there is an arc of long-established trees bordering the farm buildings to the west. Teams of horses pulling stagecoaches once used this as a stopping-off point. It is easy to imagine them swinging around in front of the backdrop of trees.

Of all the points which may make this a potentially interesting point on this track, one must consider the name itself: it is claimed that there truly are seven wells here, and that the place has been known as such since at least the eleventh century.

This may not be a particularly long ley, but it does afford particularly good views along both the ley and the surrounding countryside.

CHAPTER ELEVEN

COFFIN PATH BETWEEN NOKE AND ISLIP

As with the burial or coffin paths walked at Feckenham and Wick, both in neighbouring Worcestershire, this is an ancient right of way. Unlike the other two, which are little more than minor footpaths today, this has become part of the much lauded Oxfordshire Way.

The trackway is little more than 2km in length. It is included, not because of its length or its importance, but because it exhibits something quite unusual. The straightest part of the path is south of the line which would have connected the churches and approximately 10m up the slope. After we have followed this path we shall examine the possible reasons for this oddity.

The village of Noke has one claim to fame: it was the birthplace of Edward the Confessor in 1004. In later years, now reigning monarch, he made Noke part of the parish of Islip. It does not seem that these events were in any way connected. However, there were major implications for the people of Noke, for they now were obliged to carry their dead to the parish church of St Nicholas in Islip for burial.

Burial paths always have a starting point, a meeting place where the mourners gather before setting out on the procession to the church for the funeral. We have no reason to suppose this would not have been anywhere but the church in Noke, at the fork in the only road in or out of the village.

Today we follow this road west for 200m before following the Cotswold Way signs across the field north-west towards Islip, which is already visible. After a journey of around a kilometre, most of which is straight, we emerge on to the Wheatley Road. Crossing the River Ray, we continue on up Kings Head Lane and turn left into the churchyard.

As noted earlier, the original path seems to have run parallel to this, in a straight line between the two churches. This is not unusual, as modern footpaths are often parallel to the original tracks in order to follow modern field boundaries (this is particularly true when ancient rights of way have been lost for centuries). However, this is not the case here: no field boundaries are relevant to either the early or the modern track.

There have been suggestions that the original track was much longer, that it stretched south-east as far as Beckley. This village has the remains of a former Norman palace which not only stands next to a Roman road, but was quite likely constructed on the same site

Looking towards Islip church from Noke.

as a Roman household. This Roman and/or Norman building stands exactly on the line of the straight part of the modern track alignment. Furthermore, some 700m along the straight aligned part of the track is another former Roman site, this time a villa.

As we have said several times already, the leys pre-date Roman occupation by anything from a couple of centuries to 5,000 or 6,000 years. The Roman occupation only began just under 2,000 years ago; we also noted earlier that the Romans likely built their famous straight roads on tracks which had been laid out many centuries prior to the founding of Rome. Thus perhaps this anomalous modern alignment shows where the Roman track was built parallel to the original ley, linking the Roman houses and not the earlier settlements.

Admittedly this is speculative and cannot be proven. However, there does not seem to be any other explanation. Depending upon how long the proposed extension of the path to Beckley was in use, any evidence in the form of coinage, brooches, combs, etc. along the line between the two former Roman sites would virtually confirm this theory.

CHAPTER TWELVE

SYSTON TO ASFORDBY

Nine kilometres in length, the ancient pathway, which we shall follow from Syston to Asfordby, runs along a similar route to that from Gun Hill to Frisby. In fact, the two paths intersect, yet there is no modern junction here, nor is there any ancient marker; therefore it is not walked in this book.

The lack of any sign does not put either route in doubt, as the marker may easily have been lost or the time between the routes being laid down so great that the earlier one was unknown. Remember that these routes were already marked out by the time the Romans arrived in our island almost 2,000 years ago. Many of these will have been in use for anywhere up to five millennia, and some even longer. Thus it should not be considered surprising that some have not been recognised, particularly without accurate maps of the area or any chance of an overhead elevated view.

At Lewin Bridge the old Roman road of the Fosse Way crosses the River Wreake alongside the Gate Hangs Well public house. The road has been here for almost 2,000 years, and the river five times as long (since the end of the last Ice Age), and the route we are following came into existence somewhere between the two.

As we are completely unaware of when the trackway was marked out, it is unknown if the river crossing was in the form of a ford, a ferry, or a bridge. Although the river crossing here would probably have been all of these at some time, fording the Wreake here would have been something few would have attempted unless the river was at its lowest. There is no doubt that, even today, the river is much shallower here and there are sizable stones in the bed of the stream. Most do appear to have been worked, and are most likely remnants of an earlier bridge. It is tempting to suggest that underneath the silt and the rubble the bed of the stream still shows evidence of being a ford, though without physical evidence this must remain purely speculative.

A combination of lake, golf course and railway line means any idea of following the ley is out of the question. However, there is a clearly marked path from the bridge which follows the left bank of the river for under a kilometre until just before one reaches Broome Lane. Here the path branches – neither branch particularly follows the course of the ley, and both can eventually lead to the same place without much difference in length. I took

Fosse Way crossing the river; if it was once forded, the signs are it was possible, as it is certainly shallower here.

the right-hand path, which followed Broome Lane for a while before heading towards Rearsby just before reaching the railway and East Goscote.

One hundred metres across the field on this route we reach the railway line itself, at a point which coincides with where the path of the ley lies too. It has been suggested that a crop mark of a henge has been found on this path around this point. While it is possible, the marks were not visible while walking the route and the suggested location is a little vague. Whether it stands on this path or not is a matter for debate. As a marker we must ignore it, though it is so often cited we cannot omit it.

On the other side of the line we cross the field heading east, emerging on to the path at Melton Road. Turn left and left again at Brook Street and then forward on to Church Lane and into the churchyard. Through the church we emerge on a short road with the rather interesting name of Church Leys Avenue. Note neither the church nor the avenue is on the ley, yet the latter runs exactly parallel to it and 200m away.

Rearsby's convent is certainly on this path and a sure marker. Intriguingly it was known as Church Leys House when built in 1883 before becoming home to the Sisters of St Joseph of Peace in 1945. It should be noted that the original name of the place refers to it being built on pasture owned by the church: the reference to a ley as a trackway is purely coincidental.

Continuing on the ley, we skirt a rise west of Hive's Farm, some 3m to 5m below the summit of 78m. It is by no means unlikely that a marker once existed here: it could have been anything which would stand out against the skyline, particularly something which would have looked like a notch from afar. Our footpath takes us across the summit, affording good views on to Brooksby, then to All Saints' Church at Rotherby. Today there is no discernable marker of this track in Brooksby, although there can be no doubt that one once existed – even if the place was not settled until after the trackway was marked out. The most likely point is a crossing point on the brook, next to where the footpath continues to Rotherby, although this, even today, is tiny and would never truly have qualified as a ford.

All along the path here, which very much mirrors the original straight trackway, to the right or east above us runs the Melton Road, the modern A607, along a well-defined ridge. This footpath is easily followed, although leaving Brooksby it is as easy to take the road, which becomes better defined as we home in on the church at Rotherby; this route is known as Main Street.

All Saints' parish church stands on a rise, bounded by a wall. It is a comparatively recent and simple building, yet undoubtedly an attractive one. With the day advancing, and, before the spring equinox, with still less hours of daylight than dark, the route beckoned me along Main Street, the route we take forward. Three hundred metres along, where the houses end on the left, the road bears right. The footpath here takes us virtually straight ahead. This is the Leicestershire Round, a path which we shall be following until we reach the outskirts of Frisby on the Wreake.

Half a kilometre away we meet a junction of three lanes, together with the Round – which splits into two here, effectively giving a meeting point of six routes. Practicality means the six do not meet at a single point today, yet it is clear to see how they would have done had not the public footpaths had to make way for the tarmac which carries the vehicles between Asfordby, Frisby and Rotherby. The footpath which heads in a north-easterly direction out of Rotherby is close to the alignment, yet other than the odd meeting point the modern paths and roads do not follow the same track.

Frisby on the Wreake
stone cross.

Other than this meeting of the six routes, there are no deviations from the path or significant points on the way. It must be assumed there was something between these points at some time, yet they have long vanished through agriculture and development. Eventually fields give way rather abruptly to Frisby. The Leicestershire Round turns sharply south here, but we continue ahead along Main Street, then left along Mill Lane. The church here is not a mark point, but did make a most pleasant resting place for the last snack of the day.

Continue along Mill Lane and cross the railway via the level crossing, showing sensible caution. Then follow the footpath in the direction of Asfordby, eventually coming alongside the River Wreake and meeting up with the tarmac again at Station Road. Make use of the bridge here to cross the river, keeping an eye on the church ahead as the guide to take the correct path. The river is crossed again by means of a footbridge to Mill Lane; continue to the end and turn right at the junction along Main Street for 300 to 400m, where the terminus of the ley is found in the church.

Today it is impossible to follow the course in a straight line. In the past the river was crossed; if it was followed in a perfectly straight line today it would mean fording it no less than five times in the space of 2km between crossing the railway and reaching the church at Asfordby.

Asfordby parish church is another with a dedication to All Saints, although this is nothing more than coincidental and has no significance to the trackway. The church itself is fourteenth century, and is thus of comparatively recent construction. There is a more interesting building here, also of medieval construction. Here was found the remains of two Saxon crosses, two fragments of which bore the image of a dragon and the other a bishop with a cross. These images seem to herald from different religions. Thus, if they are reasonably close in age, they may show the transition to the Christian era.

Historically Asfordby was not a major meeting place, nor should it be seen as the traditional terminus of this ley. Indeed, its close proximity to Melton Mowbray probably shows this to have been the site of the next marker. Today there is no sign of the route presumed to have been taken by our ancestors, any surviving clues wiped away by the new industrial estates and housing developments.

Of the leys walked, this path followed the route much less than the majority. However, this did not distract from the delights of the English countryside revealed by this stroll along the course of the Wreake and of the A607 trunk road.

CHAPTER THIRTEEN

FUNERAL PATH AT WICK

We have already seen and walked one funeral path, at Feckenham. At Wick we find another, heading west to Pershore Abbey. Physical evidence of this trackway is difficult to find, but, by looking at the evidence from a different angle, it can be seen here.

As with Feckenham, Wick did not have the consecrated land to carry out its own burials, the place of worship here being just a chapel. Thus the dead needed to be transported to Pershore for the funeral. Today Wick is a small individual parish in its own right; historically it was a part of the very large parish of St Andrew based at Pershore. This is the reason for the chapel at Wick being dedicated to St Mary. However church records seem to show earlier dedications to different saints, St Lawrence in 1269 and St Bartholomew in 1479.

The path we shall be taking from here was walked for many years. Indeed, even after field boundaries and pathways were redirected, one man insisted on using the old route. The Hudson family have long been associated with the village. Around 1700, Benwell Hudson had set his sights on a life as a monk and always used the original route to Pershore Abbey to continue his studies, even though this meant climbing over fences and hedges. Obviously to walk the traditional route was very important, although for Benwell this was more likely to be from a religious perspective rather than the practical route as laid out in pre-history.

Today we are going to begin our journey at the junction of Cooks Hill and Main Street. There is no reason to think this has any more claim to being the meeting place for the burial procession than the ancient cross, yet it does fall on the alignment and junctions are traditional meeting places.

Indeed as we head west along Main Street, the first 200m are aligned with the route from the junction to the bridge. The slight dog-leg to the right has to be taken today, while the line forges straight ahead and follows the avenue with the delightful name of Timber Down, named after the Timber Croft Estate.

Continuing along Main Street we find ourselves on Yock Lane which sweeps to the right. The footpath we require heads west halfway around this long bend and heads across two fields. Across the first field we skirt the hedgerow; at the end we pass through a gate between the conifers and walk along a recently planted footpath. These saplings, suitably staked and protected by wire mesh, will one day provide a feeling of grandeur when walking this path. This would probably have been more suitable for the burial path than the modern right of way.

At the other end of the field we pass through a gate, cross a cattle grid and arrive at the river and its two bridges, one the modern road bridge, the other the ancient bridge and the site of a designated picnic area. It is the ancient bridge which is of interest, for this is where the river would have been crossed.

There is documented evidence of a river crossing here since the middle of the thirteenth century, although undoubtedly it existed before this. Indeed, the documents tell us mostly of rebuilding and repair, the first mention being from 1290 when Sir Nicolas de Mutthon left an old shilling in his will. This was to be invested and used to pay for the repair of the bridge. It is still easy to see the different colours and stonework in the bridge marking the different eras.

The first significant bridge here would probably have been built around the eleventh century, when land on both sides was owned by Westminster Abbey. Stone supports on either bank, joined by a wooden bridge, would have cost an appreciable sum of money, something the Church had in abundance.

A later stone bridge was deliberately demolished on the 5 June 1644. This was during the English Civil War, when the troops of King Charles were retreating to Worcester after the unsuccessful siege at Oxford. With Parliamentarian forces in hot pursuit, the king ordered the destruction of the bridge, itself testimony to how difficult it would have been to ford the river and provide a worthwhile crossing. However, those who wrecked the bridge were in such haste they failed to take adequate precautions, and the bridge collapsed beneath them. Forty men – including the aptly named Major Bridge – fell to their deaths, crushed by the falling stonework and/or drowned in the water. The repair, which we know was

Bridge at Pershore.

carried out before the end of that year, is clearly visible over five centuries later. This is why the middle arch has stones of a different size and colour, and is also of a noticeably different shape.

Having crossed the river, we notice something unusual for such a comparatively short trackway: it is not straight. This does not detract from the viability of the pathway: it simply shows that the river was an obstacle their technology was not yet able to overcome. The Avon is a fairly substantial river here, and even in the driest of summers it would have been a daunting task to ford such a flow of water. Thus the river had to be crossed at the easiest point, where poles could be driven into the riverbed to support a bridge.

Before doubting the ancients' ability to build a wooden bridge across the Avon, consider that there is evidence of such man-made wooden trackways running for miles across the marshlands in Somerset. Less than 70m between the solid banks of the Avon would have been a simple task by comparison.

Thus the pathway is as straight as it could be then. In fact, even today's modern road bridge crosses the river at virtually the same point and our construction techniques far surpass anything they had 2,000 and more years ago. It may well be that the river crossing marks the path of another pathway and that the Wick funeral path simply joins it here. This is the most likely explanation, but without evidence showing this other route it will have to be considered unknown or lost.

Footpath towards Wick, on
the other side of the trees.

Cross the present A44, aptly known as Bridge Street, and follow it north for just 50m before turning off on the footpath. Take the right-hand path and then almost immediately turn right and parallel the main road through the hospital grounds. We emerge at a milestone on Masons Ryde, with the destination of the abbey ahead of us.

Approaching the abbey we come to Church Street. Not a particularly unusual name for a road leading to a place of worship, yet it is the earlier name which is of interest here. Previously this was known as Lice Street, a Saxon name which does not refer to any blood-sucking parasite: this name is from the Old English word *lice*, which is very appropriate, for it means 'corpse'.

The abbey itself is of Norman construction, a still-proud ruin having suffered somewhat during the Dissolution. Evidence of earlier Saxon worship is everywhere, and archaeological studies have revealed Roman activity with numerous finds. It is likely this indicates the site has been used for worship since before the Roman occupation; a pagan temple may well have been here for hundreds of years. If so, did others transport their dead here for burial in one of the chambered tumuli associated with the period? If so, all traces have been erased, making proof of pre-Christian burials impossible.

CHAPTER FOURTEEN

BARDON HILL TO BURROUGH HILL

The start of this trackway is at the highest point in the county of Leicestershire. Standing 278m above sea level, we begin at Bardon Hill. This must certainly have been the site of an Iron-Age hill fort, though any evidence has been erased by extensive quarrying. Local legends would have us believe this was the site of one of King Arthur's great victories, when he led his forces down the slope and defeated the Saxons.

The view from the summit is less than would be hoped. Apart from the scar left by the quarry below our feet, there is a transmission mast over our heads, and the sounds and sights of the M1 motorway less than 2km from the summit. The ugliness of the modern scene is nothing like that observed by our ancestors, who marked out the track we are about to follow. However, our journey east will take us through much better scenery. It was because this point gave such commanding views that it was chosen as the starting point. Furthermore, it was walked only from here (rather than *to* here) as it was such a dreadful eyesore.

Descend the slope and head along the footpath between the trees to reach the earthwork to the east on the lower slopes just a kilometre away. This is a well-defined, almost perfectly circular earthwork, thought to have been home to an Iron-Age settlement. Oddly, no archaeology has been discovered here to add much weight to this theory. This may be for a number of reasons; perhaps it was only home to very few and/or for a short period of time.

Continuing along the now upward slope of the pathway we slip beneath the motorway and arrive abruptly at Copt Oak. Following the Whitwick Road south for 100m brings us to the church and footpath leading around it and east across the summit of the hill to Copt Oak Farm. From here it heads north-east, descending sharply along the edge of Poultney Wood and across the field alongside the brook, before heading east to Ulverscroft Lodge.

The next marker of Green Hill is now quite obvious just 800m to the east. We must take a more circuitous route so as not to trespass. The detour also gives us the opportunity to view a little more of the history of this locality, albeit a much later one. From the lodge, take the footpath heading south, bringing us past Ulverscroft Pond and the remains of Ulverscroft Priory. Neither have any relevance to the ley, but such buildings, along with the markings of the moat to the south, are of interest to any historian irrespective of the era of interest.

The solitude afforded by Charnwood Forest made it a perfect location to build a religious retreat. Ulverscroft Priory was constructed by about 1174, when it was mentioned in a Papal document. It was granted by Earl Ranulph de Gernon, who died in 1153, and early construction undoubtedly started before his death (although it may well not have been completed). It was home to Augustinian monks and stood until 1539 and the Dissolution of the Monasteries. The tower, which is still mostly intact, held a peal of six bells. The largest of these bells is reported to have been taken to nearby Newtown Linford.

Not lingering too long at the ruined priory, I continued south to the aptly named Priory Lane. Follow the road north-east from here in order to reach the next marker almost a kilometre away (if we include the short journey to the wooded hill).

Green Hill, with a summit slightly over 220m, would also have proved a challenging climb. The summit has no grand views, being largely wooded. Looking back slightly south of the route, the remains of Ulverscroft Priory were noted. The angle of the surviving walls from this vantage point meant it was seen end on. I noticed that the sun, still quite low in the sky that morning, cast a perfect shadow of the ruined wall to the north. Coming around to the east of Green Hill we have an unrestricted view of Swithland's Church, dedicated to St Leonard, just over 4km distant and our next destination.

It is a longer route around the roads and much further by public rights of way, the path of the original ley being completely out of bounds. Thus we continue along Priory Lane, descending to cross Benscliffe Road and turning left onto Joe Moore's Lane. Here the road drops down a gentle slope to turn left onto Warren Hill which skirts the hill of the same name on the right. At the end, turn right, and we come on to Main Street, heading into Swithland. Main Street is an apt name, for it is almost the only one in the village, all the properties line the road and little elsewhere. We pass virtually every home in Swithland until arriving at the church.

For some strange reason St Leonard's carries a brass plaque dedicated to Black Annis, a legendary figure known by several similar names. It seems this particularly awful individual was said to be a nocturnal female who dined on flesh and blood, being particularly fond of sheep and human children, and was said to inhabit a cave and tunnel system from here to Leicester.

It has been said that a markstone, found near the church gateway, stands very close to the alignment. Stones are notoriously difficult to prove as being markers for they are so easily moved – which was probably why this one managed to stay out of sight. This was not the case 2km further on when the three-lane junction of The Ridings meets The Ridgeway.

To reach this junction we are forced to continue around the roads, for any chance of a public footpath here are interrupted by the railway line. Out of Swithland the road crosses the Swithland Reservoir, literally passing across the southern end of artificial lake and certainly affording good views of this part of it. It is also crossed by the railway line which we pass beneath, continuing along the same road now known as The Ridings. It dog-legs across Swithland Road continuing down to meet The Ridgeway, a total round trip distance of almost 4km.

From here we continue to Rothley Court Hotel, sited on land once owned by the Knights Templar and still private property (which means there is no right of way to follow to the church). Turning right along Westfield Lane, head on through Woodgate and Cross Green to turn right on to Anthony Street; this leads to Church Street.

Rothley Church, dedicated to St Mary and St John, was built in the fourteenth century. However, there is a much older Saxon cross in the churchyard. Standing almost 3m tall, it is made from a millstone grit which occurs naturally near Cromford in Derbyshire. It is one of about fifty such crosses in the country and, as with many of these, is today headless.

The four faces of the shaft portray quite exquisite, if worn, carvings depicting scroll work, foliage and a winged beast (perhaps a dragon) and would have been most striking when it was first carved in or around the ninth century.

Standing on a grassy mound it is tempting to suggest this stone cross and not the church is the marker – though as both are so late, it seems hardly likely that either was the original signpost of the ley line. Yet it quite possible that the cross replaced the original marker, although its true origins will remain unknown.

Take the footpath and the footbridge south-east and then turn east along Hallfields Lane. Follow this road until, on the other side of the A6 trunk road, we come to the River Soar. Crossing it, drop down to the far bank of the river and follow its course in an easterly direction. This canalised stretch of the river affords passage loosely aligned with the ley through a region of lakes and pools fed by the watercourse. A pathway which follows the ley line more closely does lead away slightly to the north. However, it does make our next obstacle more difficult to pass, so remain on the bank until passing under the A46.

Here we pass Syston Mills and find a junction of footpaths. This point shows we have, once again, come to stand on the ley we are following. Here carry on north-east and under the railway line, emerging at Lewin Bridge on the Fosse Way, a point also crossed on the route from Syston to Asfordby in chapter twelve. Under the road take the left path and emerge on the A607, turning east along there for almost 2km when we come to a road-traffic island. (A minor detour into the field revealed it was impossible to see the reported crop marks revealing former barrows to the east of Syston College, although locals assured me they were quite easily seen under optimum conditions.)

Upon reaching the island, head straight across to Rearsby Road which leads us shortly to Queniborough Road, which in turn becomes Main Street and brings us to Queniborough Church. Dedicated to St Mary, the place of worship stands remarkably close to the alignment. If it has replaced an earlier pre-Christian temple site, then it seems likely the church was not built exactly on that same site. Indeed, the road also follows the ley line closely – but not closely enough – to suggest it is original. Such 'wandering' over centuries is by no means unusual, as the path of major routes still alters even today in order to avoid bottlenecks and traffic problems. The same problems existed in antiquity, although for not the same reasons, and a solution was sought.

The road from Queniborough is not the one to take, however. Immediately past the church a footpath took me up a slope to travel a ridge north of Ridgeway Farm, and from there, a long way until the next marker, generally following the line of Gaddesby Brook. The path was difficult to trace in the landscape. Eventually a combination of mud and the modern layout brought me off the track and eventually along the Ashby Road, the western approach to Gaddesby.

Turn right here and immediately left onto Main Street. After a few paces there is a footpath leading east which brings us to the Leicestershire Round. This public route has been designated to enable ramblers to take a circular route around the county of almost exactly 100 miles (160km). This route enables us to circumvent terrain which continues to make following the straight path impractical.

In 2km we come to Ashby Folville. Here, between the village and the small reservoir, a footpath leads south. Take this path and follow Church Lane, cross along Highfield End and on to Folville Street. The road twists somewhat through this course, leaving just one final sharp bend left before heading out of the village. Once this angle was almost a right angle, but it has been rounded off by planners as it was a traffic blackspot. The angle is a tell-tale clue, as this is where four ancient footpaths met, forming a crossroads. Today only the road remains, as the other two tracks are long gone. The spot where the angle once stood is still visible in the field; this point is our next marker.

We are forced to backtrack north to where we left the Leicestershire Round, continuing to follow the pathway from where we left off. After two rather uneventful but pleasant kilometres we come to Thorpe Satchville. The track brings us in at the south of the hamlet; however, the marker point is to the north. Follow first Main Street and then Great Dalby Road north until, 100m past the final house, two entrances to the fields oppose one another and mark an ancient footpath crossroads and the ley marker we have been seeking. The east to west footpath no longer exists; thus, we are forced to double back south and take the first left and back onto the Leicestershire Round.

From Thorpe Satchville the route of the Round follows the line of Bakers Lane. The modern road continues along an ancient route known as the Salt Way. This was clearly the road taken by those who traded in salt, which must have been one of the earliest commodities traded by human settlers to our shores. Two modern place names remind us of the ancient trade routes: Salter's Hill Drive in Thorpe Satchville and, back from the hairpin bend along the lane which we did not pass, the name of Salter's Hill Farm. Looking forward, we see the destination of the salt traders, one of the country's best preserved Iron-Age hill forts. The direct route is a punishing climb and, convinced the traders would have taken the easier route, this was the one I followed.

However before we get to Burrough Hill we must beware of the road doubling back. Just over a kilometre from Thorpe Satchville there is a hairpin bend with an angle of over 300 degrees. At this point there is a similar bend formed by the footpaths coming in the opposite direction. Take the left-hand path and ascend the appreciable slope to our destination.

Arriving at the upper end of the slope the view back along the Salt Way and the route

Burrough Hill.

The salter's route to Burrough Hill.

View from Burrough Hill toward Bardon Hill.

taken was as revealing as it was rewarding. Many of the markers could be made out, although there were notable exceptions closer to the Bardon Hill end of the alignment. The toposcope here points out other places of note, such as Whatborough Hill, Robin-a-Tiptoe Hill, and also the track to Old Dalby (which we shall follow in chapter twenty).

The area of this fort is somewhere approaching ten hectares. A target for archaeologists over many years, their efforts have rewarded them with findings such as the robust masonry and cobbled roadway uncovered at the entranceway. Whilst no post holes have yet been found indicating huts, a number of storage pits have been uncovered, as have various pieces of pottery, grinding stones, animal bones, an arrowhead of flint and a human burial.

This was an early Iron-Age site, inhabited from at least 500 years before the birth of Christ and possibly two centuries earlier. In order to preserve a still impressive site excavation has been kept to a minimum. It is thought to have been the centre for the tribe known as the *Coritani* or *Coritavi*, who were responsible for everything that happened in Leicestershire up to the arrival of the Romans. Indeed, the number of Roman findings here indicate the two cultures were here side-by-side, but the area was abandoned before the Empire withdrew from Britain.

In more recent times the embankments have provided a natural amphitheatre for those interested in horse racing, which was held here before the outbreak of the Second World War. In fact, it claimed that the Grand National was run here in 1873, though this was certainly not the famous horse race run at Aintree. Prior to this the man-made structure had provided facilities for villagers to hold a game and dance festival around Whitsuntide until the close of the eighteenth century.

Although the 30km should have been possible in a single day, being keen to follow the exact alignment and forced to double back and/or deviate meant walking this trackway took this author twice as long. The sights afforded by the completion made the aches and pains of the journey worthwhile. Yet it was a relief to find the car waiting at Burrough Hill, the car park being almost at the summit with the ramparts.

CHAPTER FIFTEEN

WYSALL TO DISEWORTH

This trackway takes us almost due west to Diseworth, beginning at Wysall Church in Nottinghamshire and following a line centring on places of worship. The name of Wysall is derived from the element *weoh*, perhaps telling us this was once a place of pagan worship before Christianity came to Saxon England.

Today the church is dedicated to Holy Trinity and stands on an obvious mound in the pretty village of Wysall. The vast majority of the early church can be identified as thirteenth century, with a great deal of late nineteenth and early twentieth-century restoration work.

Much of this alignment could not be walked along the original path without unacceptable trespassing across farmland. This does not suggest that the alignment is any less certain: the markers are there, but there are no public footpaths or tracks that follow the line of the ancient trackway.

It was unusual to be walking with the sun at my back in the morning, as most of my journeys tended to be east to west. It was not planned this way, nor should it be thought that those for whom these were the great highways favoured travelling in either direction. There is no right way to travel a ley any more than there is the A1 or M6.

The route actually taken between Wysall and East Leake is south of this part of the trackway: the field boundaries and paths do not fall kindly for the ley walker. At no point do we venture more than 400m from the original route, most of the time being less than half that distance. So it was a very parallel walk with repeated excursions north from the road to examine a seemingly promising region for ancient signs. Sadly, almost none were discovered, although this is not to say none exist, simply that they were not to be found on this particular day.

From Wysall we travel 2km west along the Costock Road which becomes the Wysall Road. Not considered strong enough to be a marker, the alignment does cut through the region called Little Spinney. The existence of the place and the name, seemingly unrelated to anything nearby, may indicate a marker may have stood here. Indeed, closer scrutiny reveals an old track less than 200m in length aligned perfectly. This may be all that has survived more than twenty centuries of the plough.

While we continue along the lane to the crossroads with the A60 at Costock, note that the ley converges to almost the same point. The ancient path hits the old junction, now the lay-by referred to as the Old Main Road, and from there runs north of Costock through a place called the Piggery and then hits the junction of Leake Road and the Midshires Way public footpath. Meanwhile, modern development has brought us on foot along the Leake Road to this same point, approximately 1,500m from the junction on the A60.

Leake Road's junction of paths may touch the alignment briefly just outside the village, yet it cannot truly be considered a marker (the next being the Church of St Mary's almost a kilometre further west). Once again we are only able to continue on foot along Main Street until we reach the church. The stone building is eleventh century, although there are documented records of an earlier wooden building which may have been built five or six centuries previously.

From the southern wall of the churchyard runs Station Road, a fairly common name with obvious implications. Prior to the coming of the railways, it was known as Poke Lane, a corruption of *powke*, the Saxon word for a haunting. For some a ley line and the supernatural are inextricably linked, yet whether there is any connection is not relevant here, other than to acknowledge that fact.

Coming away from East Leake, Station Road passes under the railway embankment and becomes West Leake Road. It is a total of 5km to the next certain marker. In the past there will have been other points, probably marker stones or similar. These have long since disappeared, and no amount of hunting will be rewarded. Once again this part of the route has been made difficult to follow through modern field boundaries. Yet we are given the opportunity to get away from the tarmac and walk the public footpaths which are closer to the ley.

Eight hundred metres from the railway bridge there is a footpath heading south, easily spotted for it is directly opposite the sewage works. Follow this gentle incline to Calke Hall Farm and then turn right to Manor Farm, where a left takes us down the slope to Brickyard Lane and on to the Midshires Way. The ley crosses this last leg less than 50m from the farm buildings of Manor Farm. Reaching the lane we turn right and 200m later there is a boundary hedge to the left, where we cross the ley.

This should not be considered a marker: it is simply given to show you are now standing on the original route. Look to the west and you will see Sutton Bonington just over 2km away, most of which is on the other side of the railway line. If you can make out the church you are looking along the same line as the dodder or ley marker would have looked over 2,000 years ago – a sobering thought.

Continue along the lane and head straight forward to Melton Lane where, a few metres along, we find the Star Inn. Opposite here is a footpath which we will take for 200m around the dog-leg left and then a further 100m along (this time on the right-hand path). This brings us around Glebe Farm and at once, straight ahead, the church spire of Sutton Bonington rises above the trees, coming sharply into view as we cross the bridge over the railway.

This straight road is not on the ley, despite its appearance – but Sutton Bonington Church is. Dedicated to St Michael, this is the only church on this track not on a rise. Once again the supernatural or New Age idea of leys has influenced the thinking here. On the feast day of St Michael the sun is said to set along the line laid down here – Diseworth Church is also dedicated to this saint. Although this is an interesting snippet, it has little relevance to walking or navigating the track.

The general theme when walking this ley seems to be that it was virtually impossible to follow the original line. This is particularly true of the last leg of the journey to Diseworth, for directly in our path lies junction 23A of the M1, where it meets the A42. The northern detour is the longest, and will be taken in the next chapter. Therefore we shall follow the route to the south. In effect, there are only three places on the straight section between the two churches. Slade Spinney and Slade Farm could well have been markers, as may the gentle slope to the high ground east of the motorway junction. Yet there can be no chance of finding anything today.

However, before we reach the motorway there is a much more ancient barrier in our way. The ley crosses it at a point north of the loop known as Devil's Elbow. To ford this river today would be difficult; although the levels may have been different centuries ago this would not seem likely. Indeed, the current here would also make the prospect of a permanent ferry impossible, yet without a reliable method of crossing the river it made the trackway virtually useless.

There is no archaeological evidence for a bridge, yet there are great trackways across the marshes of East Anglia and Somerset constructed almost solely from wooden posts supporting planks. If our ancestors were capable of building long trackways such as those then a footbridge across the Soar would be relatively simple. Whether such would be large enough to carry a cart – or even a horse – is debatable. Most likely the goods were man-handled across and a change of horse and cart would be available on the other side.

It would have made a more scenic route to follow the footpath along the bank of the Soar, yet time was marching on and so I decided to take Bucks Lane to the left of the church, turn left on Pasture Lane and follow this track to the canalised stretch known as the Zouch Cut. Here a bridge enables us to cross and a short step or two further along we come to Main Street and Zouch Road, or the A6006.

Turning right takes us over the river at last via the road bridge. At the end turn left on to the Derby Road or A6 and, within 100m, right along Whatton Road which skirts the lower slopes of Hathern Hill. We must take the first on the right towards Diseworth, along a lane which has several names – Hathern Road, The Green, Main Street, and West End – which takes us under the M1 and the footpath to Diseworth.

The path is well-defined in the landscape, beginning exactly where the motorway embankment ends. The path leads us across a footbridge over a brook, and up to the A42. Here we are forced to turn left to get back to the road and use the bridge to cross the major trunk road safely; thereafter follow the other side of the road until arriving at the small brook. Here the footpath continues off towards Diseworth and its obvious church steeple, visible just over a kilometre away.

The journey is quite straightforward and finally we arrive at Diseworth via Clements Gate (to be specific, St Michael and All Angels), somewhere we will be examining in more detail in the next chapter on our journey through here from near Breedon Hill to Gotham.

CHAPTER SIXTEEN

DISEWORTH TO GOTHAM

The outstanding and obvious feature in the landscape is Breedon Hill. Undoubtedly this was connected in some way with Breedon, with its quarried face which still dominates the landscape to the north-east, yet the hill does not feature in this alignment.

We start our journey north-east to Gotham in a field at Breedon Lodge Farm, exactly 1km south of the centre of Tonge. Here a square moat feature was constructed and, although just still visible, it is hidden by more trees today than it was when it was constructed. The moat was dug deliberately to encourage water to lie in the ditch, not for any defensive reasons but to reflect natural light and – almost literally – to light the way. Note that having already said that the hill at Breedon does not figure, it is highly unlikely the moat is the first marker in any ley. This indicates that there are further markers which are now lost. It seems the most likely candidate for the terminus of this ley to the south-west lay on Cloud Hill. However, whatever was here has disappeared, the land removed as part of the quarrying of the limestone here.

From the moat the ley heads off in the direction of Diseworth. The straight path taken by our ancestors is not only impractical today, but downright dangerous. Thus we head north and follow the footpath over the bridge across the A42, here turning right alongside the busy trunk road and then north towards Tonge. Hitting the lane, continue forward and take the right fork at the island, and 100m along here is a footpath leading east.

This track takes us across the busy A453 and up a slope. Around 800m along here this footpath crosses another, almost forming a fork. However, our path continues straight on, the church at Diseworth clearly visible 3km away. On the morning I walked it, the easily recognised rounded steeple stood out above the vapours of mist shrouding Diseworth, making it even more obvious. Even though there was a nip in the air on this frosty morning, the sun soon burned off the mist and the remainder of the day was a glorious late winter day under the most amazingly bright blue sky.

Soon we come to Langley Priory, a magnificent example of a manorial house dating from 1570. The trackway passes south of the house and its ponds, but the path we are following is north of the property; we are able to glimpse some remnants of the original Benedictine priory (which fell victim to the ravages of the Dissolution).

The spire of Diseworth church aligns with the old mill mound in the foreground.

Eventually we reach the lane and follow it north, continuing on to pass Wartoft Grange and turning sharply right along the pathway. Whilst this route takes us away from the path, it does give the historian the chance to glimpse what remains of the earthwork here without adding anything to the distance. When we hit the lane the church is again visible in front of us and a short walk brings us to this long-standing place of worship on its raised mound.

It was a 4km walk to this next marker, St Michael and All Angels Church at Diseworth. There are a number of the Shakespeare family graves here, former owners of Langley Priory, which was passed midway between here and our starting point. Similarly, there is a mill mound 300m after the church which again does not sit on the trackway, though it is within 30m. It is not offered as a possible marker as the date is far too late, yet may well have replaced an earlier object which showed the next point on the route.

Diseworth's church has Saxon foundations and, while the interior features quite extensive modern restoration, the main body of the building dates from the thirteenth and fourteenth centuries. Here and there some herringbone stonework can still be made out, as can the Saxon font.

From here the route takes us slightly off the actual line: the modern layout has inched a few metres north of the track forcing us to follow Hyams Lane. However, greater obstacles lie ahead which were insurmountable on foot, and so it was back to the car to navigate the M1, A42 and Donington Park Services at junction 23A. While failing to prevent the tea from dribbling down the pot onto the table as much as pour directly into the cup, thoughts turned to centuries ago when travellers did not have such problems – although they would not have had a hot drink either. Had it been possible to stand on the roof of the services' main building, doubtless the alignment would have been visible back to Diseworth and forward to Kegworth, and maybe even beyond.

The present path follows the ancient ley reasonably well, until it reaches the insurmountable modern road system. It is possible to follow these roads north and take the public footpath under the A453. From here it is north between the trunk road and the motorway for approximately 700m, until reaching the road bridge which takes us safely across the M1. This small narrow island between the busy roads is not as daunting as it seems. Indeed, the verges and islands created by our modern motorway system are home to at least as much wildlife as the ley would have been when it was first walked – not the same species, however, for there are no wolves or wild boar here today.

About a kilometre before Kegworth the gently rising slope peaks at Broad Hill, an apt name for it has no semblance of a crest at all. The ley does not cross the exact summit of 83m above sea level; however there was undoubtedly a marker here once, long since disappeared with all signs covered by the plough.

Backtracking to well within earshot of the thundering motorway traffic, the trek continued up and across Broad Hill. Today there is no visible marker here, but it is difficult to see how this shallow incline to 83m above sea level cannot have been a sighting point, for it lies in a perfect line between the churches at Diseworth and our next reference point. The ley descends from here to St Andrew's Church in Kegworth.

To follow the path along the line is, as already noted, difficult. Indeed it was decided to go to the trouble was not worthwhile. The arable land had no markers remaining and no path to follow, while the streets of the modern town have also obliterated all traces. Hence the road was followed from the A453 directly into Kegworth and the church.

Kegworth's parish church has seen many changes since its last major rebuilding work was completed in 1387. Dedicated to St Andrew, here has stood a site of Christian worship for over 1,000 years (and prior to that, for earlier religions for many more centuries). This is one of the largest parish churches in Leicestershire and well worth taking a little time out to sample its architecture. Largely medieval, some parts of the tower are from the original Norman building.

There is no route across country today; the flood plain of the river has been created to protect the town during an abnormal rise in the level of the river. Thus we take the route parallel to the trackway along Mill Lane and Bridge Fields. The bridge over the River Soar is also where we find the junction of Station Road with Kingston Lane. The modern bridge is not the original crossing point and therefore not the original marker, however the junction across the river is also slightly offline as far as our trackway is concerned. It is most likely that modern construction has made the adjustment necessary, rather than there being any error in calculations. Historically the Soar would have been crossed twice, for there is a bank or island in the middle here where the river briefly splits in two giving two channels. Here the flow of water is quite obviously reduced and fording the river is much easier.

On foot it was easier to use the modern bridge to cross to the junction of Station Road and Kingston Lane where, a few paces along the latter, a footpath heads north-east under the railway embankment to a footbridge across a minor brook and to the village of Kingston on Soar. Often the next marker is given as the church, but my calculations placed it at the junction south of the churchyard where Kegworth Road, Gotham Road and Station Road unite at The Green.

The only course open to us today is Gotham Road. As we pass over the crossroads almost 300m ahead, on the right-hand side we see a wood. From this distance it is just possible to make out the way the rounded slope juts out in the direction of Kingston on Soar. This oddly steep-sided, flat-topped hill is known as The Odells (an odd name of uncertain etymology), some 2km from Kingston on Soar. The sides are heavily wooded, but the steep rise on each side is clear enough. There is a path leading from the road along the edge of the wood, so close that there is no perspective and all we can see are the trees.

St Andrew's Church, Kegworth.

The Church of St Lawrence in Gotham.

It is not possible to climb to the top and it seems unlikely to offer any clear views of the path we have just travelled. Similarly, the only view from the other side of The Odells is also from well below the summit.

We are left to continue along the Kegworth Road to Gotham between the higher grounds on either side, finally descending into the village. Reaching the main junction, turn right and we arrive at the church. The village is best known for its Wise Men of Gotham, a series of narratives which were first seen during the reign of Henry VIII and are covered in more detail in chapter twenty. The present church is first recorded by the middle of the twelfth century and is dedicated to St Lawrence, who was serving the Church in Rome when commanded by Valerian to reveal the treasures of the Church. He brought forward the sick and the poor, offering them as the treasures through which to enter heaven. Theologically astute, maybe, but politically unwise – he was roasted alive for his actions in AD 258.

CHAPTER SEVENTEEN

HINTS HILL TO
NO MAN'S HEATH

This trackway could never be considered a major route at any stage in its history. However, even today it links two of England's major trunk roads and has a number of quite different markers *en route*. Furthermore, these markers are from a variety of eras in English history, showing both the age of the track and its continuous use.

We start our journey at Hints. Standing on the hill 120m above sea level, we face south-east and see the straight road stretching out into the distance. We are not looking along the alignment of the ley but what is now designated the B5404, previously known as the A5 and, from Roman times, as Watling Street. Turn forty-five degrees to the north and we are facing north of Tamworth Castle in the direction of Seckington and No Man's Heath. On the clearest of days the church at Seckington is visible 2km away. This is the route we shall be taking.

We shall be deviating from the original line somewhat, for 2,000 years of residence in Tamworth has changed the landscape greatly. Directly opposite us is Hints Lane, a narrow single-track road heading north-west. Down a gentle slope we pass under the modern A5 bypass and in a little more than 100m reach a footpath heading directly east. Pause here and look north-west to the woodland known as Hanging Wood (to the left), and by the extraordinary name of The Devil's Dressing Room on the right.

Halfway along this path we cross the ley for the last time until we reach the other side of Tamworth, an indication of the effect of the contemporary road system and river channels on the ancient pathway. We emerge at Plantation Lane, cross over and take the dirt track to the Birmingham and Fazeley Canal. Turn right here and follow the canal, cross it via the bridge, and continue east along Dunstall Lane.

Suddenly we are confronted by the Tamworth ring road and are about to see a number of different phases of the town's history within a few hundred metres. In truth, the route north would have been more direct, but would not have been as interesting or informative. Cross the road at the island and head off across the field toward the castle. Turn right and cross Lady Bridge, which has spanned the Teme here since the early eighteenth century, then head alongside the castle mound and up the hill to emerge in the town centre by the town hall.

The Devil's Dressing Room, Hints.

From here the street signs direct you to the town's railway station, along Market Street, George Street and Victoria Road. Facing you across the island is a small road leading past the Jehovah's Witness's church and under the railway embankment. Pass under this arch and follow the footpath along the left bank of the River Anker north-east across the Warwickshire Moor. During the Middle Ages, when it was still part of the county of Warwickshire, this was the location of a major market (hence the name). This path follows the river before departing in a straight line to emerge on to the B5493 or Ashby Road at Amington Hall Cottages. It is at this point we are standing on the ley once more.

Modern field boundaries force us to follow the road from here. A little over a kilometre along here we find the Clifton Lane heading north. It has long been rumoured on this side of the Ashby Road that this was a Roman burial site, although there has never been any official confirmation or denial.

A further 2km along we arrive alongside Seckington, a place we have already seen in chapter six. Hangmans Lane heads south at this crossroads, which is today 10m south of the alignment. However, we take a minor diversion 100m before the crossroads where, at the crest of the hill, is the remains of a motte and bailey. Seckington is a very small place today yet its earthwork remains which, with its church, are clues to it being a larger place in former times. Indeed, there are records showing this place has been around for some time by AD 757. The ley line grazes the northernmost edge of the earthwork.

From the crossroads, the Ashby Road gets closer to the track until the two connect at the crossroads formed by the footpath to the north and Kings Lane to the south. The next kilometre of the Ashby Road almost aligns perfectly with the ley until reaching the meeting point of five lanes at No Man's Heath.

The name refers to it being where the four counties of Warwickshire, Derbyshire, Leicestershire and Staffordshire meet. Indeed, the local inn is called the Four Counties.

Motte and bailey with Seckington church beyond.

Tradition has it that felons who had fallen foul of the law in one county had only to remove themselves to another room in order to escape capture. Clearly this narrative has no basis in fact, for the pub has never stood on this point but is approximately 100m further along.

As stated, the meeting point sees five lanes arriving at the point, two of which are formed by the Ashby Road, along with Ash Road, Clifton Lane and Austrey Lane. It is this last lane which is of interest. Today the modern road quickly turns south to the village of Austrey. However, the ancient path can still be seen to trace a very straight route south-east and is aligned with Appleby Hill and Norton-Juxta-Twycross beyond. It also points directly at Clifton Campville in the opposite direction. The name of this ancient track still appears on maps today as Salt Street. As we have said, salt may well have been the earliest traded commodity and one of the reasons for the paths being marked out.

The ley is said to terminate here, yet it is connected to two modern roads. It started at the A5 and could well continue on to the junction of the A444 with the M42/A42. Modern improvements have made the alignment a little vague, but it is possible to see the original path of the Ashby Road which still aligns perfectly at Little Wigston.

It is not hard to image an ancient track being marked out to connect two main roads through an important town and also coinciding with the meeting point of no less than four counties, particularly as the name of Salt Street still figures today. In truth there are few major sighting points on this ley. However, there has been a great deal of change around Tamworth and these could well have been lost. Furthermore, there is every possibility that the trackway extends in both directions, while the aforementioned line between Clifton Campville, No Man's Heath and Norton-Juxta-Twycross is also only a short length of this ancient salt route.

CHAPTER EIGHTEEN

FUNERAL PATH AT GOTHERINGTON AND BISHOP'S CLEEVE

The place where the funeral procession met to take the deceased to their final resting place, was traditionally a crossroads, although modern construction has adjusted the line of the roads here. Thus we meet at the junction of Malleson Road with Shutter Lane, though Woolstone Lane once formed the fourth path at this junction.

Many years ago Gotherington had no church or, more importantly, consecrated ground in which to bury their dead. Hence they were forced to assemble in their home village and walk the solemn burial path to Bishop's Cleeve for the funeral. Even without documented evidence we can be sure that such was a much earlier trade route, even if no trace can be found today. Here, fixed to a cottage wall, we find the sign marking the start of the route reading 'Church Walk'.

To retrace this ancient route, take Shutter Lane south; the Church of St Michael's is soon evident ahead of us. At the southern end of Shutter Lane follow the clearly marked route of the footpath. We cross two fields, the second of which parallels the last of the houses in Gotherington, when the footpath changes direction slightly along the boundary of the field. For the next 800m the modern path traces the line of the ley exactly, a fact not lost on us as the church remains straight ahead at all times. This tells us that this is both an ancient right of way and an ancient field boundary.

At the end of the field Dean Brook has been channelled to act as a drain for the springs which emerge on the flanks of Nottingham Hill to the east, on the other side of the Gloucestershire and Warwickshire preservation railway line. Follow the footpath to the edge of the housing estate where it turns right. Shortly afterwards there was a gap in the fence which appeared to have been an unofficial exit point along Nottingham Road. If this was not the case and I was lucky that day, continue on to Evesham Road and turn left, continuing on until you come to the church which gives its own directions.

However, if the Nottingham Road 'exit' point is available, follow the road south and left on Sandown Road to the junction where the church is evident once more, although approached from the opposite direction. The church is a fine architectural example, and many remaining features are Norman. The settlement is in fact much older than this: Iron-

Age pottery has been uncovered, as have Roman coins, while examples of Saxon material have been uncovered from both the Christian and pagan eras.

While this is a very short trek along a ley which, almost certainly, linked up with others and/or was longer, it is certainly an interesting one. Few have retained such a long and unbroken alignment, while none still have the sign as this one does.

Church Walk, Gotherington.

Bishop's Cleeve Church of St Michael and All Saints.

CHAPTER NINETEEN

ROLLRIGHT TO
CHIPPING WARDEN

This is almost 27km in length and a walk through some impressive parts of the English countryside. More importantly, it begins at an important archaeological site, one which must have held even higher status for those who built it.

The Rollright Circle is a group of seventy-seven stones erected in a perfect circle 32m in diameter. Correctly called the King's Men, it is associated with the King Stone exactly 73m north-east of here. A reliable record from the seventeenth century states there were just twenty-six stones left standing. As the nineteenth century came to a close those stones which were lying flat, or had otherwise been misplaced, were replaced in their original positions.

These limestone rocks have been much eroded, and some are little more than stumps in the ground while few stand higher than just over a metre. A further ancient monument is found 350m east, a burial chamber known as the Whispering Knights.

Legends surrounding the stones abound. The most often heard is that which has given the stones their name: it is said they were once human beings, a king with his army. As the conquerors marched across the land they were met by a witch who claimed she owned the land. She challenged him to take just seven steps and, should he be able to see the village of Long Compton, would be crowned king of England.

The king paced out seven of his greatest strides in that direction and looked up – but he could not see the village, for, as the witch was well aware, a barrow blocked the view to the valley below. Thus the witch turned him into the King Stone, and the men into the circle. The accompanying knights became the Whispering Knights burial chamber.

Other legends associated with a site thought to date back almost 5,000 years include that the stones, when counted, always realise a different number. It is said that a baker attempted to count them by placing a single loaf on top of each, but failed because he did not have enough – no matter how many loaves he baked.

New Year's Day is one of those times often associated with magic and legends, and Rollright has its own. It seems the stones are re-animated on this, the first day of the new year. Together they rise and march down the hill to take their annual drink from a spring which emerges at a small copse known as Little Rollright.

The Kings Stone, Rollright.

The King Stone shows evidence of wear. Indeed, it may once have been appreciably larger than it is today: not only has erosion by the elements reduced the size of this rock, but also, over the years, many individuals have chipped off pieces as good luck charms. Soldiers carried the small slivers with them into battle. Cattle drovers, some from as far afield as Wales, removed their share too.

Of course, being the major stone here, the King Stone has its own legends attached to it. It, too, is said to walk downhill to the spring at Little Rollright to drink – although the king does not have to wait until New Year's Day, for the leader has only to wait until the church clock at Long Compton is heard to strike midnight on any day of the year.

One man apparently decided to remove the stone and use it as a large block in the wall of the house he was building. Stories tell of how dreadful sounds filled the air as two dozen powerful horses strained to move the huge rock to the building. The man eventually decided to return the stone to its rightful home, something he managed to achieve quite easily with just two of his horses providing the power for the return journey.

The folklore and the history associated with this place make it a magnet for anyone with an interest in history, particularly pre-history. While Rollright may not be as visually spectacular as Stonehenge or Avebury, it is undoubtedly one of the jewels of this time. This place must indeed have been special to those who constructed it for, unlike those sites mentioned in Wiltshire, there are no other stone circles around here, only henges – and a henge does not refer to the stone or wooden construction, but simply to a circular feature enclosed by a bank and/or ditch.

The Whispering Knights, Rollright.

With such a large site, and so many markers, it is difficult to see what was intended to be the original marker. Maybe we should see this as the previous marker, for it is more likely that this was a mark point well before it had any ritual and/or religious significance. Heading off north-east it is a walk of approximately 10km to the next certain marker, although there are other possibilities *en route*. Such a distance, combined with the size of the terminal point at Rollright, tends to blur the ley somewhat. This does not help us in seeking out the interim markers, which will have existed but have been lost over the intervening centuries.

However, we have to designate somewhere as the most likely starting point, and the best candidate is the King's Men stone circle. It must be said that visibility along this line is not particularly striking from here. The line tends to follow the upper ground, giving little in the way of perspective. The way the land slopes away sharply to the north-west has resulted in the only path available to us being the road running uphill to the north-east from here. For reasons unknown, there does not seem to be any name given to this road, none appears on maps and no sign could be found along the road.

For the first 7km we shall follow the track along the road, for those few footpaths which do exist take us in the wrong direction. Thus along this lane we cross the junction with the A3400 and then turn left along the B4026. Reaching the summit at Whichford Hill there is a crossroads, both of which lie exactly on the ley. While there is no marker today, there can be little doubt that one once existed here. We shall be turning right here, but do pause to note the name of the road ahead. Beware of jumping to conclusions about the etymology of a name, for Traitor's Ford Lane may sound like it has sinister origins, but is actually a misunderstanding. It should be 'Trader's Ford' – an ancient trade route.

Shortly after turning right we descend the hill and a kilometre further along reach the crossroads known as Scotchedge. Turning north, we climb a gentle gradient for another kilometre until the only footpath along here heads east across the spring and the Sibford Road, eventually reaching the ford near Bacon Farm. Here the path we need heads back west, sweeping through the wood and then north along Hill Bottom (emerging on Grange Lane at The Folly east of Sibford Ferris). At this point we are again on the ley and, looking back, can see the previous point on Whichford Hill made clear by the avenue of trees running up the hill away from us.

Turn north-east along Grange Lane and right along Partway and the road into Swalcliffe. After the church of St Peter and St Paul, turn right along Green Lane and head forward along the footpath down to and across National Cycle Route number 5, which runs from Reading to Holyhead, and is also a much-excavated Roman road. To our right, after a 10km walk, we see our next known marker overshadowing the path.

The Iron-Age fort of Madmarston Camp at Swalcliffe is difficult to see as the plough has smoothed out much of the evidence. However, the mound stands out clearly enough above the surrounding land. The site appears to be an oval, although it is somewhat irregular and probably followed natural contours when it was constructed (although the hill itself is not particularly prominent).

Little was known of the history of the place until the first excavation in 1957, by which time there had been a great deal of disturbance. Finds included Roman artefacts, there being a Roman road south of here leading to a contemporary settlement to the east.

While the Romans certainly used this comparatively small two hectare site, the majority of its life was lived during the Iron Age. This era in human history is well named considering the items discovered during the excavation – tools, weaponry, an axe head, a sickle, a poker and iron currency bars were discovered under a stone floor.

The pottery here was coarse and of poor quality, indicating those producing the pottery were a succession of unskilled individuals (rather than all the work of one potter or examples of early work). Agriculture was clearly a major part of this community. Examination of the midden can often reveal some surprising details: there were a number of animal bones (showing cattle formed the main part of their diet) here; they also ate the meat of both horses and sheep. However, the most surprising thing is not what they ate but what they did not eat, for there is not one single pig bone to be found.

Ahead of us we can see the aptly-named Round Hill. After a tiring walk the prospect of this climb was daunting, yet there was no alternative route and we ascended to within 20m of the summit. As I rounded the hill on my trip, the welcome sight of Shutford was below me, the pointer of the church being somewhat less welcoming than the George & Dragon, which provided a welcome resting place and more than adequate refreshment.

Turn right at the Church of St Martin's and follow the Banbury Road east to Five Ways. Take the second road on the left to the north-east, heading down past Beggar's Barn and then taking the path through the trees and gully known as Padsdon Bottom to pass the next marker (Castle Bank) at the southernmost corner.

The origins of this earthwork enclosure are shrouded in mystery. There is no early documented evidence and archaeology has little chance as farming methods have left little obvious remains. Aside from aerial photographs (and the bank still visible around the hedgerow) there is little to see. The site is very square, which has led some to suggest it was a temporary Roman fort. However, this is pure speculation, and without further evidence it will simply be a mystery waiting to be solved.

Continue along the footpath; All Saints' Church at Wroxton is now visible on the hill. The footpath crosses the lane and heads towards Wroxton College, once Wroxton Abbey.

Our route takes us north and joins Dark Lane, where we turn left and continue forward along Church Lane to the next marker.

Our alignment passes through the corner of the tower. This part of the fourteenth-century church was rebuilt just over 200 years ago. There is documented evidence of an earlier church on this site, although no physical trace of it remains today. The church is the last resting place of Frederick, Lord North, who served as prime minister for two years from 1770. Shortly before his death in 1792, he took the family title Earl of Guildford, whose ancestral home is now the aforementioned Wroxton College – a school for American students in Britain.

While the ley line heads off in a straight line for 7km to the north-east, our path heads north along Church Street to Silver Street and then right where it becomes Stratford Road. After a kilometre we have passed over the infant Sow Brook, and arrive at the Roebuck Inn. Queens Crescent heads off north and leads to a footpath which takes us through the embankment of the former railway line and on past the lakes of Drayton Lodge and the golf course. Emerging at Warwick Road, the footpath crosses directly across the road, across Gullicatte Lane and heads toward the Church of St Peter at Hanwell.

Hanwell's church is not a marker and, although the ley passes directly through it, neither is the castle – actually a late fifteenth-century fortified manor house by William Cope. We shall not dwell here, for the sights are not relevant to the ley, while the sounds of our next major modern obstacle of the M40 motorway have been heard for some time. Pass west of the church and head north to yet another pub, the delightfully named Moon & Sixpence.

Turn right on Main Street, which becomes Hanwell Road and crosses the motorway before climbing again to the A423.

There is a footpath which we could take to the south, leading ultimately to the valley of the River Cherwell (which also contains the canal and its Oxford Canal Walk). While this would make a pleasant change of scenery and bring us to the same place, it does take us further away from the original ley than the modern roads. As we are walking an ancient track as much as possible, we should reject it in favour of the latter, slightly less scenic, route. So turn left along the A423, then right along The Close and Station Road through Great Broughton to arrive at Cropredy. Here, turn right along The Plantation and the bridge over the canal to reach our next marker, the crossing over the Cherwell.

This small village just to the north-west of the delightful River Cherwell is so named because the place was originally an ancient river crossing, a ford across the shallowest part of the river. Indeed, this point is also where two leys cross, the other known as the Waterstone ley. Despite the name of the village, as far as we can tell the first bridge was not constructed here until 1312.

The most famous moment in the history of Cropredy Bridge happened on 29 June 1644. As any historian will know, this date is an important one in English history, for at that time the English Civil War was splitting the country in two. The Parliamentarians were under the command of Sir William Waller, whose other claim to fame is as the man who proposed the formation of the New Model Army where professional soldiers fought under trained officers. Prior to this, the troops were composed of any able fighting men, led by aristocrats whose only qualification to lead a war was through their bloodline. Opposing Waller were the Royalist forces, under the command of King Charles himself.

Here reports are conflicting. Some speak of a fierce battle, while others maintain it was only a minor skirmish; both agree that the Royalists were victorious, which marked a milestone in the history of England – for this was the final battle won on English soil under the command of the reigning monarch. The different descriptions of the encounter come about because they were written by different sides. The ferocity of the battle is exaggerated by the Parliamentarians: defeated, they wished to tell of how bravely they

The historic Cropredy Bridge.

fought. However, their opponents describe a virtual walkover where hardly a shot was fired in anger.

So which is correct? The answer is found in the addendum to the Royalist record. It speaks of their disappointment at how their victory realised so very little, for their prisoners were not the cream of the fighting force and the captured equipment well-nigh worthless.

Whilst I decided against following the canal and the river before Cropredy, we can now do so, for it takes us to a point on the ley. Double back to the canal and follow the Oxford Canal Walk north. Some 70m after the lock gates, a footpath heads east alongside the Cherwell past Prescote Manor, and thereafter north-east.

The river is with us for over a kilometre, although we continue on for another 500m. Here the path swings right and we can see the village of Chipping Warden in the distance. Ascend the slope (keeping the village ahead of you) and it will keep you on the right track, which is not particularly evident on the ground. This is sadly true of the last marker on the ley.

Within 60m or 70m of the road ahead of us on our left there is an earthwork known as Arbury. Its existence would likely never have been noticed were it not marked on earlier maps, for it is virtually completely ploughed out. The field in which it stands has a rather oddly shaped funnel-like projection leading to the road, while the western boundary is also shown as an embankment known as Arbury Banks.

Clearly this was once a substantial site noticeably larger than the present village of Chipping Warden. What is known is that this represents at least two eras in history. The larger banks are part of a medieval field enclosure system, while the smaller earthwork is Iron Age or earlier. The latter is of most interest, for it is on the alignment. It would be interesting to know more about this site, who was here and when. Unfortunately, further information will now be extremely difficult to find.

All that is left of Arbury Banks.

The modern reminder of Arbury Banks at Chipping Walden.

This was a rewarding walk which took me two days to accomplish, extended to a third day as the author took a leisurely stroll back along the Cherwell and the canal from Cropedy back to Banbury. This was not part of the original plan, nor is it of any relevance to walking the ley. Yet it did provide the ideal opportunity to enjoy the warmest day of the year so far and was the perfect way to recharge the proverbial batteries.

CHAPTER TWENTY

BURROUGH HILL TO OLD DALBY

B urrough Hill is both one of the highest points in Leicester and a well-known hill fort dating from the Iron Age. The finishing point for the walk of chapter fourteen, the history of this important site is discussed at the end of the walk from Bardon Hill.

Interestingly, we can actually still discern the notch in the bank of the hill fort. This was a favourite method of marking a ley when possible, as the artificial feature stands out clearly when silhouetted against the skyline. Looking through the gap from the top of the hill to our target of Great Dalby's church does not have the same effect as the reverse. However, remember to glance over your shoulder when journeying to St Swithun's, for it is quite surprising how clear the marker appears when seen from below.

Make for the northernmost corner of the fort; there is a toposcope at the top of a flight of five or six steps which shows compass points if required. At the rim of the ramparts here the hill falls away sharply along a well-worn path skirting the woodland to the left. Follow this path down and around the trees and our destination, Great Dalby church, can be seen directly ahead of us, 3km away.

At the edge of the woodland the slope becomes less steep and heads towards four or five farm buildings, crossing Burrough Road in the process. Turn right and walk along Moscow Lane for 700m, then take the footpath left to join Little Dalby Road towards Great Dalby. Cross straight across the lane known as Woodgate Hill and follow the paths there, keeping an eye on the church so you don't become lost around the somewhat tangled paths here. This will bring us to Main Street and St Swithun's.

The church has been here since the early thirteenth century. It stands on a slight rise in the village and is a well-kept building, although its architecture and monuments offer no assistance in tracing the line. Leave the church and descend the slope to join the lane known as Top End. In the absence of any helpful footpaths, follow this lane north-west. Cross the railway and pass Eye Kettleby, roughly paralleling the ley until we reach Leicester Road.

Turn left here and head east for 600m and you will see the next check point, and a most unusual one at that.

It is over 3km from the church at Great Dalby until this next point of interest near Kirby Bellars; a mound here on the corner of Leicester Road at Kirkby Park (opposite

Thorpe Satchville Road) has a Scots pine growing from it, seemingly deliberately placed there. This is a common enough marker in the south-east of the country and, while not quite unique in Leicestershire, is not found often. Its almost artificial appearance may be deceptive, and the tree's location quite natural. If there is a marker it is certainly not the original tree, though it may be that successive generations of the original tree have been encouraged to grow. Without further evidence, we must suggest it as a possible marker.

It is another 2km until we reach All Saint's Church in Asfordby. There was a choice of routes, none of which were favoured by the original alignment. Hence, the option I have suggested is simply the most scenic. From the tree, take Main Road north-west and turn right on to Main Street. Continue over the railway and the road runs out. There is a footpath to follow, turning initially west around the churchyard and then right past the site of the former priory.

The clearly marked footpath follows the field boundaries before following the embankment through the pools and alongside the River Wreake. Eventually it reaches Station Road, where we turn sharply right and cross the river and a couple of channels via the footbridges. This is the only path here and it brings us out at Mill Lane. Turn right on to Pump Lane, then right again on to Asfordby Place where we reach the church via All Saints Close and Church Lane.

Most of the building was from local stone in the fourteenth century. However, there is a Saxon cross-shaft inside the church here, depicting a bishop holding a cross and a dragon. Thought to be tenth century, this could well be the best clue we have to show the existence of an earlier marker post.

Head north along Church Lane and turn left along Main Street. Just after the road bends to the right, turn off along Saxelby Road. Passing under the A6006 Loughborough Road 250m later there is a footpath heading north-west. Climbing a stiff slope we reach the summit and find another footpath crossing the one we are following at right angles. This meeting place of the paths marks the next marker on the ley line. None of these modern footpaths have any relationship with the original ley we are walking. The contemporary routes have been influenced by the way the land has evolved under the influence of mankind.

Just north-east of here is Saxelbye Tunnel, which allows the railway to pass through the ridge upon which we are standing. It is interesting to note that the road, the tunnel and the lodge are all recorded as Saxelby, the suffix from the Old Scandinavian *by* meaning 'village'. However the village is misspelled 'Saxelbye', which has influenced the name of Saxelbye Wood, Saxelbye Park and Saxelbye Road Farm.

From here the land undulates gently for around 2km towards Grimston. Luckily there is little deviation in the direction of the footpath, making it easy to follow over the brook and up the rise to Saxelbye Park where the church at Grimston can be clearly seen, providing us with a visible target. Indeed, this path we are walking is so close to the original pathway as to be almost indistinguishable on a map, although this is not the case on the ground.

The path leads past Wembley House and onto Church Lane. Here the Church of St John the Evangelist stands on an appreciable mound and was once part of the large estate of the Knights Templar centred on Rothley. In the 1990s, excavations were being carried out on the drainage system when a one-and-a-half metre long stone was found buried a metre down near the tower. How or why it was here is unknown; it is almost certainly the mark stone which predated the church. It can never be suggested as being the original marker for the ley, yet may well have marked the meeting place for the pre-Christian pagan ceremonies.

The final leg of the journey, 2km of inclines, is virtually impossible to cross directly today. In the earliest days a wealth of minor markers would have led the traveller from

Rothley Church.

Grimston to the Church of St John the Baptist at Old Dalby, or the contemporary marker occupying the same position.

Take the path which continues behind the church and note how closely we are paralleling Perkin's Lane. This path brings us out on Six Hills Lane, which we cross and continue along through Old Dalby Wood. The path rises and then falls slightly toward Old Dalby's church, bringing us to Paradise Lane alongside the church.

Today Old Dalby could never be considered a major place. Thus it is hard to see how it may have been the terminus of this ley. However, at the time the leys were being marked out, anything from 2,000 to 8,000 years ago, the size of the present village would have made Old Dalby a sizable place.

In truth there is no reason to believe this is the termination of the ley. Possibly the route continued to meet the forerunner of the Roman Fosse Way, or maybe that road had not been marked out and the track headed across to Widmerpool, 7km away, and even beyond. Without hard evidence to substantiate this, we will likely never know.

CHAPTER TWENTY-ONE

THRUMPTON TO
THORPE ARNOLD

This is a south-westerly track leading from Nottinghamshire and across Leicestershire. We begin at Thrumpton, known to stand on the Trent at a vital crossing point in pre-history and opposite the former Roman road to Derby.

Thrumpton church of All Saints stands opposite the fine Jacobean architecture of Thrumpton Hall and is somewhat overshadowed by it. The church stands on a noticeable rise, the land here being just 30m above sea level. However, that rise is nowhere near enough to give a view of the next marker. Even standing on top of the tower at Thrumpton, the tip of St Lawrence Church at Gotham is still invisible.

From the church we head north toward Ferry Farm for 100m in order to pick up the present-day public footpath. The path describes an arc to the bottom of the slope of Gotham Hill, crossing Barton Lane and the A453 trunk road in the process. Where it reaches the point at the bottom of Gotham Hill we are briefly back on the ley. Today the footpath climbs the hill at an angle, thus avoiding the one-in-ten incline of the original ley, yet it is still a tough climb.

All of the ley lines followed in this book have lost a significant number of their markers. What is unusual here is that the position of the lost marker is known. Without clear line of sight between the two churches, the only place for a marker was on the top of the intervening ridge. It is clear this ley must have had a marker on top of the 97m high point in Gotham Hill Wood on Cottagers Hill. The climb from Thrumpton is a steep one, roughly corresponding to Cheese Hill, Gloucestershire, made famous by the cheese rolling featured in the stories of the Wise Men of Gotham (first published during the reign of Henry VIII).

The story tells of how a man from Gotham was travelling to Nottingham market with a sack full of cheeses. He rested often on his journey, lastly at the top of Gotham Hill. As he stood up, one cheese slipped from the sack and rolled away down the hill. Thinking his wares were anxious to reach Nottingham, he rolled the rest of his cheeses after the first, meaning he was no longer forced to carry the heavy load.

Of course the cheeses ended up in bushes, hedgerows and ditches. However, he waited all day at the market and, when they failed to turn up, realised his folly – they had of course not stopped at Nottingham, but continued on to York. So he hired a horse and set off in pursuit. As darkness descended he was seen racing away to apprehend his cheeses.

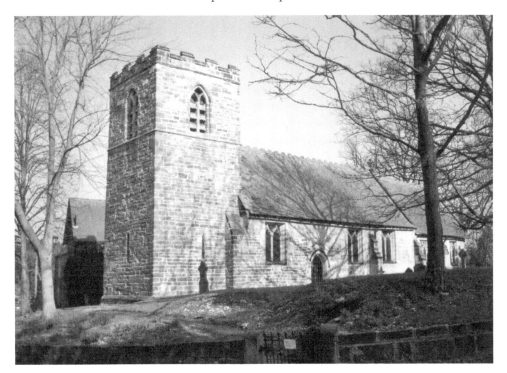

All Saints' Church, Thrumpton.

Today it is still difficult to see both churches from the same point, as the trees here (roughly at the midway point of the 3km between the churches) obstruct the view one way or the other. Our destination is the Church of St Lawrence at Gotham, the termination point of a ley already walked in chapter sixteen.

Following the path through the wood, it emerges at a point where four other paths merge. Only one heads in the direction of Gotham, now clearly visible without the trees in the way, and from there down the steep slope and along the straight path to emerge on Kegworth Road alongside the school. Here turn left and forward to the junction where looking right will show the church.

Just over the road from the church is the Cuckoo Bush public house, which is said to be (along with the churchyard) where ghosts have been reported. There is said to be a tunnel between the two, although this has never been found. A second tunnel was also said to exist between here and the Manor House which, when discovered, would contain a hoard of gold coins. A passage was discovered in quite recent times, yet there was no record of any treasure trove located within.

From the church, head east along The Green and bear right, following Moor Lane; shortly after a right-angle bend in the road to the left, and about 80m along on the right, we rejoin our footpath. The junction between Moor Lane and the footpath is as close to being on the ley as it is possible to show. Follow this footpath, branching left after about 200m and shortly following the bed of a dismantled railway. Eight hundred metres along here, the path turns sharply to the right and then sharply to the left at the footbridge over the small drain. Straight on we pass under the Great Central Railway preservation line and through Welldale Farm to join the Gotham Road and the Midshires Way – a connected network of footpaths, bridleways and quiet country lanes linking Princes Risborough in Buckinghamshire with Stockport in Greater Manchester.

Bunny Hill Top.

The ley line hits the Gotham Lane at this self-same point. This is the first of a number of times when the modern recreational footpath will meet the route of this ancient trackway. While we follow the Midshires to the A60 and turn right to climb the hill to the top, the ley takes the more direct route up the testing incline of Rough Hill. This small but steep rise to 80m above sea level has no signs of any markers, yet it is almost certain one existed here. The location provides good views over the route of the ley, and reasonable views of the alignment to our next major point, the delightfully named Bunny Hill.

The marker here is formed by the hill itself, not a peak but a notch clearly visible from the north. The original notch was at Bunny Hill Top, the route of the original road here. Today the notch in the ridge is even more obvious, for it has been cut below the original level to accommodate the busy A60 trunk road.

The name has nothing to do with lagomorphs, but 'dry ground in a marsh where reeds grow', from Old English *bune* and *eg*. The trackway does not reach the top of Bunny Hill, but climbs to around 85m, approximately 7m below the summit. Making use of the Midshires Way again brings us safely through the wood. The irony of the modern route providing an easily traced alternative route through woodland is not lost on us, for the first ley lines were created over 5,000 years ago to enable our ancestors to do exactly the same thing. Descending the gentle slope we soon emerge from the woodland and our next sighting point, Holy Trinity Church at Wysall.

It is 2km along the Midshires to Wysall, an easy walk through open farmland, our target of Holy Trinity Church in sight with virtually every step. The church clock is imaginatively designed to honour the twelve inhabitants of Wysall who saw action during the First World War, all of whom returned home safely.

Holy Trinity Church at Wysall.

The church has a distinct spire, easily recognisable from well back along the path. Work on the church began in the latter part of the thirteenth century, with much restoration work carried out during the Victorian era. It stands above the surrounding buildings on a mound and is thought to have formerly been a pagan shrine prior to the arrival of Christianity.

The Midshires continues over Main Street directly opposite the church, and for 50m further along the trackway mirrors an older footpath (which covers a distance of some 400m). About a kilometre from the church we cross a footbridge spanning the young Kingston Brook, then 500m from here meet up with the brook again (which mirrors the course of the Midshires for almost 2km). We pass through the district known as Thorpe in the Glebe, from Old English 'the outlying farmstead in the muddy district'.

By the time we reach West Thorpe Road at Willoughby-on-the-Wold we have been forced to stray from the ley. Thus we need to cross the road and take a few paces north where, at Old Hall Farm, the local church shows the footpath to take. Arriving at Church Lane, follow it around until it reaches Main Street, where we turn right and follow this around to Back Lane, and turn left towards the Fosse Way. The map shows a footpath here which would enable us to cut off the corner. However, the distance saved is marginal and, despite a search, I could not trace this path on the ground.

Four kilometres from Wysall along the ley we reach the A46, still better known as the Fosse Way, as stated previously named from the road with the ditch. The Roman road parallels the modern trunk road here, separated by a maximum of 70m. Here Back Lane and Station Road form a crossroads very close to the summit of the hill. The alignment passes through a barrow, which was where annual festivities were said to have been held during the eighteenth century. Archaeologists excavated the site thoroughly prior to its destruction when the interchange was constructed.

Near the junction was the site of the Roman town of Vernemetum, sometimes given to mean 'the grove of spring' or alternatively 'the great sacred grove'. Either way, it seems it was formerly the site of pagan worship during Celtic times and the reason for the original marker. Nothing can be seen today, although there have been a number of discoveries by metal detectorists.

There is little opportunity to examine the original path of the Fosse Way, as what remains has been covered for some time and the evidence long buried. Take the loop around and over the trunk road: it is the safer option and the slightly elevated position gives a view along the original Roman road which, when conditions are right, may just be made out.

Having returned to Station Road, follow it for 200m and then take the footpath south. This will take us south-east to Nottingham Lane on a course roughly parallel with the ley which crosses the ridge above us at the appropriately named Longridge, not far from its highest point of over 120m and where there must have been a marker in antiquity.

Continuing forward along Nottingham Lane, turn left on to the lane known as Longcliff Hill, then right on to Main Road until its junction with Paradise Lane where we are, once again, back on the original line of the ley. Looking back in the direction of Wysall we can see the steep descent the ancients would have taken down Longcliffe Hill itself.

We are forced to meander once more away from the original ancient path, although we will be crossing it quite soon. Just 80m east take the footpath leading up an ever-increasing gradient. After 400m a second path crosses which should be taken, aiming to pass to the right of the summit, a slightly less daunting ascent than that of the path we have just left. This takes us along the slope of Green Hill and affords good views over Old Dalby after crossing the railway and skirting Marriott's Spinney to the south. Eventually the footpath brings us to Ostler Lane, where we turn right to reach the crossroads at Green Hill, the next marker on our ley.

Here the point sees the Ostler Lane to Saxelbye crossing Six Hills Lane. The latter is a Roman road, so named because it is the point which links with the Fosse Way at Six Hills, 5km south of where we crossed it. Although this crossroads at Green Hill has no known evidence of Roman construction, it does align perfectly with the stretch of the ancient road of Six Hills Lane and also the known stretch of Roman construction still 3km to the west. It is known that this route was an ancient salt way and could possibly have followed an earlier ley line.

We only came along Ostler Lane to the crossroads to meet up again with the ley and take advantage of the good views to check if any of the sightings can still be discerned. There is a choice of routes here (either to return to where we left the footpath at Ostler Lane and continue east, or to follow the lane east from the crossroads). Both converge at a single point. However, one affords views, while the lane route does not. Both bring us to the same point on Six Hills Lane at Berlea Farm where we find another path leading south-east and views to Wartnaby.

The modern route is going to take us over half a kilometre away from the original ley, though the terrain means our walk gives good views over the ancient pathway. While our ancestors would have taken a route through Saxelby Lodge and Marriott's Wood, we head around Friars Well Farm to the south then follow Spring Lane and the footpath which gives clear views to the Church of St James at Ab Kettleby. This is not our target, however, for when we reach the junction we head directly east along Main Road and then after 100m take the footpath south-east.

Although we are now walking below the summit and with elevated terrain all around, we still have quite excellent views and in particular to the south. This is a stretch of a 1.5km and, after we have crossed Welby Lane, through a jumble of footpaths. There is little point looking down here, as this will simply confuse. Look straight ahead and a valley gives views up to Potter Hill; for confirmation there is a line of trees along the brook which trickles down through here. This is the path to follow until reaching the Nottingham Road.

From here the scenic route forces us way off the ley line, hence in order to mirror the ancient trackway as much as possible we head south towards Melton Mowbray. It is a walk of over 2km along the A606, which ascends to cross Potter Hill where the elevation affords some good views, especially toward the south, and it is worthwhile pausing to take in.

Archaeologists discovered a number of burials here, possibly dating from as early as the Neolithic period. The bodies were all aligned facing east, and for some gruesome and inexplicable reason, all their legs had been broken following their deaths. It has been suggested this shows the people were enemies and this was to prevent them reaching the afterlife. However, this has one major loophole – it was simply unheard of for the enemy to be buried by the victors at this time.

The town of Melton Mowbray doubtless had a marker once upon a time, yet whatever it was has long since disappeared beneath the concrete of the north of the town. It may be lost beneath the modern construction, yet there are glimpses of potential remnants, as we shall see.

Entering Melton, the modern buildings begin to the west some 600m before they do to the east. At the point where St Bartholomew Way joins here, we once again stand on the ley itself. There is no suggestion that this was in any way a marker, however it is merely given as a reference point.

We must continue until reaching Dieppe Way, turning left for 200m and then following as the road turns sharp right. Take the first left (Ludlow Drive), then left again at the end along Scalford Road; 300m further along, turn right along Wymondham Way, right again along Longfield Way, then left along Granby Way to enter Melton Country Park. The irony of trying to follow a straight line marked out over 2,000 years ago via such a complex and tortuous winding route is not lost.

We are now in sixty hectares of parkland and lakes purposely constructed for leisure activities. A popular location for locals and visitors alike in warmer months, we have emerged facing a natural ridge which provides a path between the lakes. It is tempting to suggest this is a natural feature and this ridge has been here for thousands of years. While there is no doubt there has been a ridge here for some time, it is impossible to find topographical maps showing contours or the lie of the land much more than 200 or 300 years old. Just how much it formed a part of the ley is uncertain; however, that the trackway falls along the southern edge of this ridge is certain.

Cross this ridge and follow the footpath running south alongside the disused railway, which can be crossed via the old tunnel and leads on to Doctors Lane. Continue until you reach Ferneley Crescent, which is followed round to its end, turning right on to Bowley Avenue, and then left to follow Thorpe Lane. As the road bears left we are once again on the ley line, as this road now runs alongside the alignment for half a kilometre. Indeed what is now Thorpe Bridge must once have been where the brook was crossed by a ford and/or a small footbridge.

To our right along here, the fields show clear evidence of earlier occupation, while the earthworks in the last field are still clear, as is our next marker straight ahead of us. Once a pre-Christian place of worship, it is today known as St Mary's Church at Thorpe Arnold. Standing on a pronounced rise above the valley to the west, it overlooks Melton Mowbray. The church was built in around AD 1200; the font is Norman and features a knight with raised sword taking on four dragons. The earthwork to the south-west is all that remains of the original Iron-Age establishment, although there is clearly some much, much later construction dating from medieval times.

Here the ley concludes, a distance of about 27km from the start at Thrumpton. However, the detours have probably made the journey closer to 40km. Much of the original path has disappeared, although we were still able to follow the rough line enough to see that, even today, it covers some fine English countryside. Admittedly this was also a route which covered more tarmac than most, yet the contrasts between the two undoubtedly added to the experience.

CHAPTER TWENTY-TWO

OAKHAM TO GREAT CASTERTON

This is an alignment which follows a path of 16km from the county town of Rutland to the east. It was among the shortest of walks and yet one which afforded the loveliest of views, particularly as we skirted Rutland Water. Indeed this man-made lake has infringed upon the ancient trackway at one point, forcing us to divert around its waters.

It was an overcast spring morning when I began the day at Oakham's Church of All Saints. The 50m spire of this impressive parish church dominates the skyline of Rutland's largest town – in fact, it is easily the largest church in the county. The present church was constructed in the fourteenth century, although there were two earlier churches here, and it is certain it had been the site of religious worship for many years earlier.

The route we are attempting to trace heads almost directly east. Effectively next door to the church is Oakham's best known feature, its castle. While often referred to as a castle, it should strictly be described as a fortified manor house of which only the great hall remains. Indeed, it has been described as the most complete English hall in the country by none other than Nikolaus Pevsner in his *Buildings of England* series. Much of the earthworks are still visible today, while the whole community are encouraged to enjoy the site with a children's playground, skateboard area, flowerbeds and bandstand in the grounds.

For the last five centuries there has been a tradition of a forfeit due from royalty whenever they passed through the town. Payment was made in the form of a horseshoe (which explains why there is such a large collection of these items within the hall). Oddly, they hang upside down, which is generally considered unlucky; however, hanging it this way is said to prevent the Devil from sitting in the hollow. Whether the hall can be considered to be on the ley or not is never going to be answered, as it is simply too close to the church. The only logical answer is to regard them jointly as potential markers.

For simply practical reasons we shall begin at the church and follow the Viking Way and Hereward Way, routes totalling over 400km and giving access to the Lincolnshire coastline. These names give the ramblers' routes a romantic air – somehow the official European designation of E2 seems clinical. We shall not be travelling far along the route; it is simply the simplest and most scenic way out of Oakham.

Oakham's Buttercross.

Take the path north-east out of the church/hall position, which brings us to a staggered junction formed by Station Road, Vicarage Road, Ashwell Road, and Burley Road which we shall continue along in the same north-easterly direction. A little over 100m along here we turn left along Woodland View which leads in a straight line through the housing development to a tree-lined route and out of the town. The lane crosses Burley Park Way and turns sharply right at Dog Kennel Cottage. After about 50m on the way toward the sewage works we cross the alignment and eventually reach the road where we turn left.

This is the A606 – which also serves as part of the Viking Way and Hereward Way, which we have met before – and the cycle route 63. It is also a part of the Macmillan Way, a route sponsored by the cancer research group marked out between Lincolnshire and Dorset. It is not a single path but has a network of side paths off the main route. Monies raised by those walking the routes in the form of maps and other sponsorship go to Macmillan Cancer Support. Whatever name or designation is given to this way, it is the only one we can follow around the north-west shore of the reservoir.

When it was opened in 1976 it was the largest man-made lake in Europe. Over thirty years it has grown from being simply a source of fresh water into an important wetland nature reserve and one of the principal leisure centres for the area, popular for boating, fishing, bird-watching from the shore in purpose-built hides, or walking and cycling around it. There are two centres for cycle hire, near Edith Weston on the south shoreline and Whitwell to the north. Without any footpaths to follow to Great Casterton, it was necessary to use the roads. Thus I decided it head for the cycle hire south of Whitwell.

Heading east along the A606 the path routes runs parallel to the road from about a kilometre onwards. When eventually reaching Burley Wood, look south along the shoreline of the reservoir and you will see two small promontories; the second is where the trackway begins to cross the reservoir, and soon we shall be standing on the line almost exactly where it reaches land again. It is approximately a further kilometre along that the leisure route veers to the south, away from the A606, and we should follow it to walk the shoreline around the region of Barnsdale Hill.

As we zig-zag south along the path we approach the water once more and, 100m short of the shoreline, we cross the alignment. From here the route swings east, meandering around between the shore and Barnsdale Wood along a well-marked route to reach the cycle hire point at Whitwell. This is where I collected the bicycles in order to finish the journey to Great Casterton by pedal power. While this may not have been in the spirit of walking the ley, it was impossible to walk, so I decided to take advantage of this alternative method of transport.

From the hire centre we turn left and head north up Bull Brig Lane, a leisurely ride up a gentle gradient. It is a ride of less than 600km to the next marker, which stands just before the corner; turn right along the trunk road once more. Whitwell Church is dedicated to St Michael, the only one in the entire county. Beneath the chancel is a holy well, although in earlier pagan times this would have been referred to as a sacred spring. In fact it is this very water source which has given the place its name on the 'white well', probably indicating an association with a water goddess. The church stands on raised land adjacent to the A606 to Oakham and has some delightful stained glass.

Turning east we continue along the Whitwell Road; after a kilometre we pass the butterfly farm. If there is time, this is an excellent tropical showpiece, featuring birds, reptiles and snails which are allowed to roam freely along with the butterflies. There is also a display of aquaria featuring fish indigenous to the Rutland area, although not exclusively the reservoir itself.

Great Casterton church.

Continuing east, we eventually come to Empingham and turn left along Main Street which takes us straight through the village. The last lane on the right is Mill Lane where, looking a few metres along, we see buildings on either side which show where the ley line crosses. A short way after the junction the Rutland Round, another leisure route, enables us to continue off road. An initial climb levels off and then drops gently as the route turns toward the north-east. There is a fork where the Round splits from the footpath: for those who are uncertain, the right-hand path is the correct one.

Four kilometres after leaving Empingham, we enter Tickencote. It is not on the ley (indeed we are now some 600m north of the alignment), but is as close as modern pathways allow us to get. There is only one route through this tiny village, yet it does take us safely across the A1 or Great North Road to Great Casterton. Meanwhile, the ley forges across country directly through Ingthorpe. There is no evidence to suggest there was ever any marker here; the place is as large now as it ever was, consisting of just a few farm buildings.

We follow the line of the Old Great North Road, down and through the village to the church and the Plough Inn nearby. Great Casterton's parish church, dedicated to St Peter and St Paul, used to stand on the A1. However, this major arterial road now bypasses the village and the church now officially stands on the Old Great North Road, known from Roman times as Ermine Street. The Romans had a town here, itself built on the site of the temple dating from well before the Romans arrival.

While this ended the ley, I was able to enjoy a light yet welcome snack at the local before returning along the route to return the bicycles and await our appointed collection time. Luckily for my companion and me, the car was held up in traffic and we were able to enjoy the delights of what must be among the nation's loveliest man-made creations.

CHAPTER TWENTY THREE

DROITWICH TO ALCESTER SALT WAY

Any road, be it modern or ancient, exists for the sole reason of getting from one place to another. As noted several times in the previous pages, one of the first reasons for travel was to trade salt.

As hunter-gatherers, man fed from the land, he followed trails which he knew would feed him and every meal was fresh. Yet 10,000 years ago, following the last Ice Age, the first farms appeared around the newly founded permanent settlements. In order to preserve their meat they rubbed salt in and dried it. Unlike other products, salt was only available in a few places, such as the famous salt works of Droitwich. Indeed, this is exactly what was meant by the Roman name for the town, *Salinae*.

Man would have soon realised the potential for trading salt for almost anything they desired. The network of tracks which were marked out between these early settlements is often still preserved by way of the names of contemporary roads. Look at virtually any town today and there will be a 'salt' name somewhere. This is particularly true of Droitwich, which has a Salt Way as long as any in the land, and has a huge brine lake beneath the ground.

The Roman occupation of Britain has traditionally been said to be the period when straight and well-made roads first crossed our island. There can be no question that the quality of the roads was very poor before the arrival of the great empire. However, there is increasing evidence that the surveying had been done centuries before, including the clues here around Droitwich.

There are at least four Roman roads known to radiate from a single point in the town. The best known is the A38, also referred to as the Icknield Street, which runs north-east to south-west. From the north is Crutch Lane, which also partly doubles as the leisure path known as the Wychavon Way. Finally there is the Salt Way, the path we shall be following, which heads to Alcester and another major Roman road known as Ryknild Street. The point in the town is at the crossroads of the Bromsgrove Road, Worcester Road, Hanbury Street, and Saltway and adjacent to the River Salwarpe.

These Roman roads were once thought to have been constructed as the means to transport the salt. This theory does not stand up to close examination, for there was

The saltway from Feckenham to Droitwich.

certainly brine being extracted well before this. If the brine was being drawn then it was being taken to be evaporated for its mineral content. There are other sources in the country, yet none have such a concentration as is found at Droitwich – it is claimed only the Dead Sea has a greater degree of salinity.

This is not to say the Romans did not up production here. In fact we know that salt was not only used as a preservative but was also given to their soldiers who could use it as currency. This is the origin of the word 'salary', paid to the soldier who was clearly thought to be worth his salt!

Our target is Coughton just north of Alcester, and in particular its junction with Ryknild Street, some 20km to the east. Any thoughts of following the exact alignment are, for the most part, out of the question. There is a certain irony in the original path being obliterated by first the Roman and then the modern routes, so closely do they follow the original trackway. Despite the straight road, intervisibility along this path is not possible.

Beginning at the Droitwich crossroads, we head east along Hanbury Street, then Hanbury Road under the motorway to arrive at Hanbury Wharf. From here the road once again returns to its original name of Saltway, something we shall find again and again along the route today generally referred to as the B4090.

Reaching the railway line, look back and notice how it is possible to see Droitwich, now over 2km away, yet the M5 is difficult to make out, as is the Worcester & Birmingham Canal just 500m away. Even more striking is the church at Hadzor on a hill just a kilometre away, which appears obvious. This is perfect proof of how even the lowest marker will stand out in a predominantly flat landscape when it looks quite different. Both the motorway and the canal are many, many times larger than the anything at Hadzor – and yet the eye is drawn to it.

From here we continue along past some interesting names to the south, including Gallows Gree, Cross-in-Hand and Crowle View, none of which are relevant to the ley. Arriving at Mere Green we turn off the path, heading straight ahead as the road diverts north. Head straight on at the sewage works, through the trees, and follow the field boundary into the next field. Then turn right. Skirting this field, we climb the hill and head straight over it; at the summit of the path, again look back along the track, for this point is perfectly aligned, before descending the slope to and across the point of the field facing us along the line of the path.

Diagonally across the small triangular field we arrive at a hedge and brook: cross it and head to the lane beyond. Turn left along this unnamed lane to the corner and there turn north-east to rejoin the Saltway at Brook Farm, the brook in question being the Seeley Brook. This cross-country walk has avoided the loop of the B4090 towards Hanbury, which is a modern anomaly and has nothing to offer to the trackway we are following.

Continue east along the road once more until arriving at Feckenham, a burial path we walked in chapter eight. Here the track briefly becomes known as Alcester Road for a distance of less than 200m between the side roads of High Street and Moors Lane. A kilometre after Feckenham we pass Rockhill Lane on the left. From here the Saltway performs a series of uncharacteristic loops and bends to head between Wheating Hill and Shurnock Court, swinging again at Lower Tookeys Farm and at Hall View.

It is fairly obvious that from Glebe Farm the line of the Saltway is not aligned with straight road which was left at Mere Green. There is but one explanation: the modern road known as the Saltway has been influenced by later routes as the importance of Alcester grew. Yet the original path, used before the Romans were ever seen on our shores, headed directly for Coughton.

Hence we leave the modern road opposite Shurnock Court and take the footpath across the lower slopes of Wheating Hill. On reaching a second footpath turn south after 200m to the brook; then turn east once more 50m on. There follows a quite complex series of footpaths intersecting with our route and one which sadly offers no target by line of sight. However, it does stick very closely indeed to the alignment; even field boundaries have altered the route little. (A compass is helpful to help prevent us from straying away from the correct line, and to locate the right path.)

We find ourselves topping this small rise north of Lower Tookeys Farm before climbing the short, but to the left of the woodland and straight on, take the left fork at Manor Farm to reach the oddly-named Edgioake Lane. Cross straight over and follow the southern field boundary to cross the Monarch Way footpath, and turn right 100m later. We are now walking a gentle slope parallel to the road known as The Ridgeway. We are shortly able to head toward this road alongside the small copse.

Across the road the ridge of land drops down via a footpath to Whitemoor Road, where we turn right and find ourselves at an island. From here a footpath leads across the field and into the woodland. This is Coughton Park, a region historically known as Dark Dale, a somewhat unkind name for a delightful walk through woodland offering welcome shade on a warm day at the end of a tiring trek. The sounds of the woodland here cannot be greatly different from what was heard by those who first walked here many centuries ago, for the trees dampen the sounds of modern civilization until we emerge on the other side into the light once more.

From here the footpath followed the edge of the woodland, reaching Sambourne Lane where we turn right. This road leads us down to Coughton itself and the remains of an ancient cross on the line of the Roman road of Ryknild Street. The village of Coughton is best known for the Tudor House, home to the Throckmorton family since 1409, and is closely associated with the story of the Gunpowder Plot. However, there is much older history literally in the road outside, which invariably gets overlooked.

Ancient cross, Coughton – said to be where travellers stopped to pray for safe passage through the Forest of Arden.

A most enjoyable walk which could only have been improved by greater visibility along the line itself. To have walked along an original known Saltway was a worthwhile and quite moving experience. Unlike many of the routes this book covers, this was comparatively flat. The terrain – combined with the shorter length and the temperature – make it a sensible choice for a warmer day, especially with the shade offered by the woodland toward the end.

CHAPTER TWENTY-FOUR

BUXTON TO CARSINGTON

To be accurate we are north-west of Buxton at Long Hill. Standing on this well-named road 300m above sea level affords good views over the Fernilee Reservoir and the Goyt Valley.

The terrain is going to make following this track extremely difficult, especially in the earliest stages. We will be following a line created many years ago, today marked by a number of field boundaries, footpaths, trunk roads and the route of a Roman road. Our path will take us as close to the original line as possible, whilst also keeping in mind this is a leisurely stroll through history, one designed to be enjoyed with a minimum of physical exertion.

Tearing our eyes away from the view across the valley and to Hoo Moor, we head south along the road also appropriately known as Long Hill. A little less than 2km there is a hairpin bend, the road following the contour from Rake End. Here we leave the road for a while, taking the Old Longhill Road down the valley, across the stream and up the other side to a field boundary.

Crossing this stile, pause to note the route this boundary follows. East of here the boundary wall turns sharply and parallels our path in a south-easterly direction. Despite the optical illusion created as the line runs down to the road and then up the steep incline away from it, this wall runs perfectly straight for exactly a kilometre. The line passes right over the exact summit of the hill 456m above sea level and descends to Brookfield beyond. While a field boundary is not considered a normal marker, to have a wall in perfect alignment along the ley for such a distance, to have it cross the highest point, to not follow any known political boundaries, and to ignore contours makes it stand out.

By crossing here and continuing upwards along the same road, we will come close to the line once more. Here rejoin the modern A5004 and continue south-east until, 700m along, pause at the field boundary on the left and note the position, for this is on the ley line once again. Shortly afterwards, we reach the junction with Old Road, which follows the path of the early Roman road and is the line of the modern Midshires Way route of 360km.

Passing Cold Springs Farm, the road name changes to Manchester Road, telling us

Looking west across Fernilee Reservoir.

where the road is heading (in the opposite direction), and continue along to reach Buxton. Entering the famous old spa town, we turn right on to Park Road and head forward into the park itself. The park has no relevance to the walk but is well worth the slight detour to take in the landscaping and the sight of the famous opera house.

We exit the park via the south end of Park Road, shortly arriving at St Johns Road which, although it marks the line of the ley once more, cannot be said to be a realistic marker point. Continue forward along Burlington Road to the next junction, turn right along Bath Road and then immediately left along West Road to the crossroads of five roads (which stands on the alignment). Here take the right along the A515 or London Road, following it until we reach the junction of Heath Road (which is where we cross the ley once more). We shall keep following the A515 south until we come to the cemetery on Ashbourne Road on the left.

Ahead of us lies a straight line of road of no less than 3km which aligns perfectly with the ley. Further markers are found in the shape of two road junctions: that formed by the crossing with Heathfield Nook Road, and where Buxton Road joins from the south at Brierlow Bar.

Running alongside this stretch of road for the first half this part of the walk is the line of a former Roman road. From the junction at Brierlow Bar the same Roman relic runs on across country, and yet it does not take much to realise this not is not the famed straight Roman road. Somewhere in the break of the visible track, the Roman road bends at an angle of approximately thirty degrees. While the modern roads follow the ley, the Roman road very much mirrors the route but cannot be said to lie on it. Looking at this makes it easier to see how today's roads follow the ancient routes rather than the Roman ones.

We continue along the A515, for not only does it offer the least physically challenging route, but also the closest path to the original ley at this stage. Just over 2km along from the

Cronkston Low there is a tumulus on the summit.

last marker, we arrive at Great Low. Here, opposite a milestone, is a tumulus at Great Low. It is not a marker, as it is some 400m north-east of the nearest point on the ley and 40m above our heads. However, it does stand on the crest of a hill, which would have made it quite prominent when it was first constructed. Thus whilst not a marker as such, it would have been an excellent confirmation point alongside the ley.

Across the other side of the A515 is a line of eight fields. Down the middle is a dividing boundary line which lies exactly on the track, showing how it orients itself in the landscape and helps us to recognise the earliest route. Seven hundred metres further along, just after the quarries and Downlow Farm, we leave the road and travel south along the Midshires Way to join the High Peak Trail and the Pennine Bridleway. They are all the same route, and converge here to make a single track – or more correctly, this way is used by all three routes.

After 400m the High Peak Trail turns ninety degrees to the left; pause at this point and look south-east. We are not high enough here to check the alignment behind us, and we are some 50m or so north of the track, yet in front is the 400m plus high Cronkston Low with its tumulus. While this was undoubtedly associated with this trackway, the marker lies on the lower ridge 500m beyond this and visible to the left. Today there is little to distinguish this place from the surrounding scenery, but when this was a route in regular use there would have been a quite obvious marker here.

Head east to follow the High Peak Trail which swings around south-east and runs parallel to the former Roman road and the A515, whilst also narrowing the gap between the original ley and our present path. The path then takes us straight ahead through Sparklow, where the Royal Oak offers excellent refreshment, across Tagg Lane and over a crossroads. Two hundred metres after the crossroads there is an unremarkable point, marked by nothing, but which is where we meet the ley once again.

From here our path continues to wind its way along following the contours around

Cotesfield Farm and between Custard Field Farm and Moscar Farm, once more crossing the ley. Meanwhile, the other side of Moscar Farm the A515 has been following the Roman road for 700m before turning to the right to avoid a tumulus which the Roman road well-nigh bisects. We shall be examining this Roman path later, for while here it clearly has no relevance to the route we are walking there is every chance it does follow a different path closely associated with this one.

Back on our path we pass a promontory at Darley Farm. These buildings stand on the original trackway. Again, this farm is not suggested as being a marker, simply as an easily recognisable point of reference for following the ancient trackway. Soon afterwards we find the High Peak cycle hire centre at Parsley Hay; here, for a few pounds, a bicycle can be found to help to explore the 50km of mainly flat trails. This is one of a number of stations where excellent refreshments are on offer. Indeed, the aroma of the bacon as I passed proved irresistible.

Another 400m along the paths split, and we take the left-hand path and soon meet up with the A515 once more. This crossing point is not on the ley: that crosses the trunk road 50m north of here and meets our path 200m further on. It is just over 3km along the trail to the next marker. After crossing Green Lane, we arrive at the brick works and Friden, where the crossroads fall within a few metres of the ley. The original marker would have been easily seen, for while this is not the summit it is on the side of the hill and any artificial marker would have stood out against the skyline.

It is over a kilometre straight ahead along until the route turns south and meets the A5012 at Newhaven Crossing, the next marker point. From here the journey continues around the dismantled railway, following the contour on a gentle path through Gotham and across Parwich Lane. Two hundred metres along, after crossing Mouldridge Lane, we converge with the trackway once more.

Looking ahead along this straight section of the High Peak Trail, on the ridge 300m away, is a tumulus. There is no suggestion that this would have had any connection with the ley we are following, although it may well have had connections with a similar ancient construction which did once stand on or alongside the ley line. Similarly, 1,500m south-east, on the slopes of Minninglow Hill, are three further constructions which may also be secondary ritual sites.

Aside from the two tumuli on the slopes, there is Minning Low itself. This is a prominent cairn 40m in diameter which has four distinct chambers and shows several phases of construction. The present construction has remained unchanged since the Bronze Age, although the earliest is from the Neolithic. As with many hill-top sites, it is marked with trees. Here a ring of beech trees make this site stand out from below, even though the ancient site itself is invisible from here.

Below the hill at this point are a number of disused quarries alongside the High Peak Trail. It is at this point where the ley crosses our modern path, just where the path takes the first of three left turns until we are heading east. From here it is just 200m to the next marker on the trackway, which happens to coincide with the boundary of the National Park and a parish boundary. Boundaries such as this exist for a reason, and are notoriously difficult to move, thus it is certain that a substantial and important marker once existed here and for some considerable time too. Just what form that marker took and when it disappeared will remain a tantalising mystery.

Continuing further along this path we arrive at Longcliffe. Pass this tiny hamlet to the west over the road and at the next road crossing, south of the place, follow the road south towards Brassington. Ignore the left turn along Manystones Lane and drop down into the village. At the fork take the Kings Hill to the right and keep your eyes west of this lane. Just 100m away, just below the summit on the slope of the hill, is a tumulus. Only visible from the road under certain conditions, this ancient burial mound lies exactly on the line of the ley and is a certain marker. The site is known to consist of an earth and stone tumulus and the remains of two stone cairns, which suggests it was once a site of some importance.

Shortly afterwards we arrive at the junction of Kings Hill, Church Street and Miners Hill. This junction does lie exactly on the ley and Miners Hill indeed follows it for a few metres. Whilst there is no suggestion that this is another marker, today these roads are of little importance; it is quite possible it had some significance. As we come down Miners Hill, ahead and slightly to the left is the summit of the hill between here and Carsington Water. Undoubtedly a marker, such as a pile of stones, once stood here, although no sign of anything remains today.

Today it is not possible to walk anywhere close to the summit of the hill between Brassington and Carsington Water along the line of the ley. Hence I decided to take the more leisurely route along the road to the south, if only because the length of this walk was already quite punishing. Furthermore, the ley remains as distant from the route no matter which route is chosen. Thus in Brassington we head south along Town Street, continuing on for 2km where a short track enables us to cut off the corner and head east along the B5035 Carsington Road.

No directions are needed to the reservoir: simply find the most advantageous point and enjoy the site. Opened by Her Majesty Queen Elizabeth II in 1992, this is the ninth largest reservoir in the country. Much excavation had been carried out in the decades before the valley was flooded. Evidence of human habitation for at least 4,000 years has been found, including a burial mound, human remains, and an assortment of flint tools. Behind us is a journey of over 30km between two of the most impressive sights in and around Derbyshire.

On our journey I made reference to the former Roman road and, as promised, we are returning to that road to examine the line it cut across the Derbyshire countryside. It has

Carsington Water.

been stated elsewhere in this book that Rome built its roads straight and did so on the tracks marked out hundreds or even thousands of years before. We left the Roman road as it went almost through a tumulus north of the A515 and Moscar Farm. As stated, the road does not run at all straight but describes an oddly zig-zag line across the land as much as the modern trunk road does.

The number of pre-Roman sites it joins up from this point undoubtedly suggests the track existed prior to AD 43 when the Romans arrived. That it is an ancient right of way is also shown by the way the fields treat this as a natural barrier, rarely crossing it at all. Indeed a glance at a map might make the line of the Roman road appear to be a fault line in the earth's crust, so well defined does it appear. It is this line of field boundaries which we shall be following, although it is not recommended as a practical walk unless one is prepared to face a number of charges for trespassing!

North-west of the A515 the Roman route runs directly through Middle Street Farm. Place names with the element 'street' or 'strat' always refer to specifically Roman roads. Follow the line of the field boundaries south-east (note how this boundary is a perfectly straight line, and yet the boundaries do not line up on opposite sides of this line). It crosses the lane known as Long Rake where, on the other side of a small copse, is the remains of a tumulus. This is the first of several pre-Roman markers and shortly we find evidence of another place name to refer to Roman influence.

Across Green Lane is Manchester Plantation, the suffix comes from Old English *caester* referring to a Roman fortified place. Within 200m is another tumulus, this time standing virtually on the road itself, close to the crossroads formed by the lane running south-west to Friden. From here the line of the fields is more broken, the line of the road not formed by the field boundaries as sharply as before.

However there is a wealth of minor place names which are known to have been favoured as markers on these early tracks: names such as Holly Bush Farm at Pikehall, a tumulus again near Nine Miles Plantation, the aforementioned Minning Low and its associated tumuli, with yet another such burial site on the projected path of the road as we approach Longcliffe. After this the road is blurred and uncertain, lost beneath modern development, both agricultural and rural.

Without doubt the two tracks were related in some way. While it would be easy to see them as running alongside each other, enabling travellers to cross this part of Derbyshire without getting lost, in truth they were unlikely to have been in use at the same time. It seems likely the Romans constructed their road on the track in regular use at the time of their arrival, in which case the ley line we traced in this chapter would have been rarely used (if ever). This means the ley in this chapter would probably have pre-dated the Roman road by at least 2,000 years and most likely at least twice that time judging by some of the sites discovered on the route.

The Roman roads of England are less than 2,000 years old. Stonehenge, the epitome of the ancient site across the western world, was completed 4,000 years ago. It is a sobering thought that some of these leys could be over twice this age. No wonder the tracks are so well worn into the landscape.

CHAPTER TWENTY FIVE

GREAT WITLEY
TO DROITWICH

As we have already seen, Droitwich was an important centre since it was discovered that a brine reservoir existed beneath the town. By evaporating the brine an important and precious commodity was produced – salt. We have encountered the salt ways leading from Droitwich elsewhere in this book, normally walking from the source rather than towards it as we will be here.

Our journey begins east of Great Witley, north of Stanford on Teme and overlooking that river from the summit of the aptly named Round Hill. Visibility along the ley is difficult – indeed it is likely that this continued much further west. However, modern construction has made tracing this extremely difficult and, for this reason alone, we begin at this point. Our first destination is clear: just a little to the south of direct east is Walsgrove Hill. At 250m it is over twice the height of Round Hill and will prove a challenge to the unfit when we arrive there.

First we must descend 60m from the tree-covered summit of Round Hill, to negotiate the first major obstacle on our path and cross the previously mentioned River Teme. This tributary of the Severn meanders through a valley which it has helped to create. A rather large river to be forded, it would have been crossed by way of a rudimentary wooden bridge created by driving heavy wooden poles into the bed which supported the planks on which the travellers crossed. Today we shall use the modern Stanford Bridge 400m downstream. The footpath skirts the summit of the hill where we descend south-east to a small brook, a minor tributary of the Teme, crossed via a footbridge and join the B4203 to head east across the river.

At this point we are as far from the original route as we will get, approximately 400m. From here we could take the series of footpaths to the north of the road, yet these are steep paths leading through woodland and quite difficult terrain. Furthermore, it is a tortuous winding course which repeatedly leads us towards and away from the road, offers no views of the ley itself and drastically increases the distance we would travel. Thus we will, at least until the next marker site, be walking along the road.

After crossing the Teme there is a public house, well-named The Bridge, which affords excellent refreshment for those travelling this route in the opposite direction and nearing

Looking west to Round Hill from Walsgrove Hill.

Lambing time on the slopes of Walsgrove Hill.

the end of their journey. During the very wet early summer of 2007 the river rose almost to within touching distance of the bridge. Pause to observe the valley here and, assuming the waters have receded, the volume of the river in spate can be imagined. Clearly in times when travellers had only horses and a wooden bridge, the crossing would have been impossible, even suicidal.

We continue along the winding route of the B4203, climbing steadily for 3km. At the crest of the hill there is a lane heading south: some maps give this as Walsgrove Lane, yet the Ordnance Survey map does not name it and for the brief period I was on the road there was no sign of a name. Here the Worcestershire Way leaves the lane a few metres from the junction. Follow this route up the hill; the summit, between the two groups of trees, affords excellent views to the east.

While there is the splendid former residence of Witley Court, two sizable ponds and a main road, the major marker which stands out here are the greenhouses at Hillhampton Farm. Indeed these greenhouses belong to the farm where there would certainly have been a marker stone or similar for many years. Today there is no sign of anything, which does not mean none exists: either it has yet to be discovered or (more likely) it has been moved.

Although it does not feature as a marker on the ley, the views from Walsgrove Hill are enough for us to appreciate the splendour of the estate and we cannot pass without mentioning Witley Court. This nineteenth-century stately home would probably be referred to as a palace today, were it not for the devastating fire in 1937. There are magnificent stone fountains, one of which has been restored, and work continues on restoring the building itself. Even if the building itself is little more than a shell, albeit an impressive one, the grounds laid out by William Nesfield still maintain a breath-taking magnificence, particularly in the spring when the rhododendrons are in bloom.

In order to reach this next point we have to double back along the footpath from Walsgrove Hill to turn east along the B4203, 800m along turn right on the A451 and, if you can resist the temptation of the Hundred House Hotel, take the A443 right fork opposite this establishment. It is a walk of over 2km to the farm near the junction which was seen from the viewpoint of Walsgrove Hill.

We continue along this road as it descends a gentle slope. Just over 1km along here is an interesting place name, even though the place does not lie on the ley line today. It is quite possible that the name, which refers to a general area, originally referred to a place some 200m to 300m north of here. The name in question is Dodoak; an oak tree was a favourite marker for it was long-lived and the largest single entity available to those who created the leys. The name given to those who marked out the leys is often said to be dodmen, or dodders. While there is no certainty of this, it is very tempting to point to the name of the farm buildings here as evidence of a nearby trackway.

It is a further kilometre along this road before we turn off along the footpath to the north. There are two such paths: one is marked as turning off at Sankyns Green Farm, but I was unable to find this and walked 200m further along to the well-marked lane north. It sweeps around to the right and meets Rectory Lane at Shrawley. Turn right and 80m along come to a three-way junction which falls exactly on the alignment. Here would have been where several roads converged, a meeting place, possibly where the traders were met by representatives and where they distributed the precious salt.

At the junction follow the road to the left and then turn right along the B4196. Three hundred metres along here we cross the original track once more. Here there is a footpath heading south to the churchyard and the remains of an ancient cross. Once again we are tempted to suggest this replaced an earlier cross which may have once stood further north. Doubtless we shall never know if this is the case, yet it is an intriguing thought.

The next great barrier is the country's longest river, the Severn. Follow the route directly and there stands a smart and welcoming establishment which tells us how our ancestors overcame this problem, that of the Lenchford Hotel. The name of the hotel is taken from the place which, by the twenty-first century, has all but disappeared from maps and roads with the exception of the hotel.

The first element of the name is from Old English *hlenc* which is a side form of *hlinc* and is seen as meaning 'hilly' or possibly 'slope'. The latter definition would fit this place perfectly, with a second element speaking clearly of the 'ford' which provided access across the river. Today the prospect of crossing the river on horseback or horse-drawn vehicle is enough to concern even the bravest, even when the river is at its lowest. Just how our ancestors viewed this leg of the journey can only be guessed at.

Today the nearest means of crossing the River Severn lies to the south, downstream at Holt Fleet. Thus it is here we shall be aiming for before continuing our journey. As luck would have it, the B4196 takes us south to the A4133 where we turn left at the crossroads and follow the trunk road across the bridge.

On the opposite bank the road sweeps around to the right, thereafter passing a footpath on the right leading past a large number of static caravans. Opposite here is the footpath we require, leading north-east to bring us to Uphampton Lane directly ahead of us. This lane rises to Uphampton itself and the second junction along this lane. Standing here, before we turn right, note we are at the next marker point and at a road junction which has remained unaltered for centuries.

Continue along the road and, after it describes a very odd V-shape for no apparent reason, it becomes Woodhall Lane and brings us to and across the A449 where it is thereafter known as Haye Lane. This road runs for over a kilometre in a perfectly straight path and falls on the alignment so precisely it must be all that remains of the original trackway. When the lane turns left it runs directly south-east for 300m and there is a footpath heading toward the quite obvious Nunnery Wood. However some 100m before the wood the path swings right and shortly afterwards joins up with Monarch's Way. Here we turn right and head through Westwood Park toward Droitwich.

North of us here is the site of the former Westwood House. While anything here today cannot possibly have any relation to the ley, it is almost certain that the site was chosen as it already had some significance. What is here today is a splendid brick Jacobean house standing behind what some would describe as an even more impressive gatehouse.

The land here in Westwood Park is flat and a gentle stroll as we approach the end of our journey. Having passed close to the northernmost tip of the Great Pool, turn left on the lane and walk through the woodland to Westwood Way; turn left and shortly afterwards right at the traffic island along Briar Mill, which takes us over the A38 trunk road, the River Salwarpe and the Droitwich Canal.

Here we turn left along Ombersley Way to cross the railway. At the island the road continues to the right until it meets the Saltway. Here we turn left and follow it around until we can turn left and cross the railway and the river once again. Church Lane is on the left and St Augustine's is already obvious. This is the oldest church in Droitwich, the present building started in 1180 and completed within fifty years although a wooden Saxon church was here before this. In truth it does not stand on the ley but is within 30m of it. Such a distance is acceptable, there could well have been an earlier pagan site here which was marked by a stone – indeed the stone could have been utilised in the foundations of any of the churches constructed here.

Another interesting clue here is the hill on which the church stands, which is known as Dodderhill. As noted, just before we reached Shrawley there was the place name Dodoak. Here is a similar name where the first element gas been given as referring to the parasitic

St Augustine's Church, Droitwich.

plant dodder *Cuscuta epithymum*. Often seen as red string-like threads running across the ground, it is found in grass and heathland. This red colouring shows how the plant lacks chlorophyll, which makes plants green and is the catalyst which enables plants to produce their own food. A lack of chlorophyll is a good indicator of a parasitic plant, although it is not it is not conclusive. Some of these plants can have threads many metres in length – the potential combined total length of all the threads from one plant is quite surprising.

Any suggestion of Dodoak being named after the plant would be dismissed fairly quickly as lacking any real evidence. However, the name of Dodderhill is most likely a reference to the plant, for the evidence seems to date the place name as being from the Saxon era. There are plenty of examples of place names being misunderstood, particularly where there are two different languages involved. In this case there would be a Saxon word referring to the plant, while the man who surveyed the ley line – also known as the dodder or sometimes dodman – would have been from the Celtic group of languages or possibly earlier.

There is no doubt it would be nice to think this was the place at Droitwich where the dodders or dodmen lived and worked, particularly as there are a number of trackways emanating from Droitwich with it being a source of valuable salt. Dodding would have quickly become a skill which was much sought after and the individuals themselves well respected and admired members of the community. This was inevitable when they were the community's only lifeline to the outside.

The very straight Haye Lane between Great Whitby and Droitwich.

This was a walk of 20km across Worcestershire from the foothills of the west near neighbouring Shropshire to the valleys of the Teme and Severn in the east as we near Warwickshire. Along the way we have seen some quite different aspects of the county. While there is little visibility along the ley – the elevation is simply not great enough – it does offer glimpses of the trackway, particularly along Haye Lane.

It may not have been the most scenic of walks, nor did it have the most history. However, it did have an excellent standard of licensed premises and, while not all were sampled during the walk, they were all visited at a later date.

ACKNOWLEDGEMENTS

In the preparation of this book I would like to thank all those who aided me in my research and my journeys.

Before a single step was taken there was the help from: the librarians across the Midlands their assistance in providing maps old and new; Ordance Survey, without whom I would soon have been lost; and those who have suggested some of the routes in the past.

Thanks also to those who provided refreshment and a place to rest, while turning a blind eye to muddy boots and soaked clothing, the inevitable result of the unpredictable British weather.

Most of all my thanks to those whose local knowledge meant I avoided taking many a long route.

The lovely Dovedale, the perfect resting place on the route in Chapter 4.

Other local titles published by The History Press

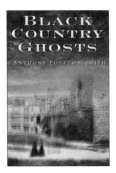

Black Country Ghosts
ANTHONY POULTON-SMITH

Local author Anthony Poulton-Smith takes the reader on a fascinating
A–Z tour of the haunted places of the Black Country. Contained within
the pages of this book are tales of spectral sightings, active poltergeists and
restless spirits appearing in streets, inns, churches, estates, public buildings and
private homes across the area. This new collection of stories is sure to appeal
to all those intrigued by the Black Country's haunted heritage.

978 0 7509 5044 2

Leicestershire and Rutland Place Names
ANTHONY POULTON-SMITH

This dictionary of Leicester and Rutland place names examines their origins
and meanings. It includes not only towns, villages and hamlets, but also
rivers, streams, hills, fields and woods, as well as streets, buildings and public
houses. A comprehensive description of the origin and evolution of each
name is given, which brings to life the history of the place in a new and
remarkably revealing way.

978 0 7509 5045 9

Derbyshire Place Names
ANTHONY POULTON-SMITH

This dictionary of Derbyshire place names includes districts, towns, villages,
hamlets, together with notable buildings. A comprehensive description is given
of how each name originated, thereby bringing to life the rich tapestry of
history that has shaped Derbyshire over the centuries. Essential reference for
the tourist or local historian, Anthony Poulton-Smith's book will be absorbing
reading for everyone interested in the names of Derbyshire's towns and villages.

978 0 7509 3925 6

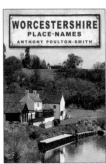

Worcestershire Place Names
ANTHONY POULTON-SMITH

Few of us are aware of the implications, symbolism and history of the
names we use every day, or indeed of the continuous process of naming
and re-naming that goes on around us. This comprehensive dictionary of
Worcestershire place-names, their origins and meaning, includes a full
description of how each name originated is given, thereby bringing to life
the rich tapestry of history that has shaped Worcestershire over centuries.

978 0 7509 3396 4

Visit our website and discover thousands of other History Press
books.**www.thehistorypress.co.uk**